Make That Grade
Marke ing

Third Edition

Margaret Linehan and Thérèse Cadogan

Gill & Macmillan

Gill & Macmillan Ltd
Hume Avenue, Park West
Dublin 12
with associated companies throughout the world
www.gillmacmillan.ie

© Margaret Linehan and Thérèse Cadogan 2000, 2003, 2007

978 07171 4206 4

Print origination in Ireland by Carole Lynch

*The paper used in this book is made from the wood pulp of
managed forests. For every tree felled, at least one tree
is planted, thereby renewing natural resources.*

CONTENTS

DIAGRAMS

TABLES

1
INTRODUCTION TO MARKETING

Chapter objectives

After reading this chapter you should be able to
- define marketing
- trace the historical development of marketing
- identify the elements of the marketing mix
- understand the marketing environment
- understand relationship marketing.

1.1 *Marketing defined*

This chapter begins with an examination of what is meant by the term 'marketing'. Kotler et al. (1996) has defined marketing as 'a social and managerial process by which individuals and groups obtain what they need and want through creating and exchanging products and value with others.'

The definition of marketing given by the British Chartered Institute of Marketing is: 'Marketing is the management process responsible for identifying, anticipating and satisfying customers' requirements profitably.'

The American Marketing Association's definition of marketing (AMA, 1985) is: 'Marketing is the process of planning and executing the conception, pricing, promotion and distribution of ideas, goods and services to create exchange and satisfy individual and organisational objectives.'

These definitions show that
- marketing is a management process
- marketing is an activity geared towards giving customers what they want
- marketing identifies and anticipates customers' requirements
- marketing fulfils customers' requirements efficiently and profitably
- marketing facilitates exchange relationships.

Marketing occurs when people decide to satisfy needs and wants through exchange. *Human needs* are a state of felt deprivation, for example basic physical needs for food, clothing, warmth, and safety. *Human wants* are shaped by culture and individual personality. Wants are described as objects that will satisfy needs: for example, a hungry person in the United States might want a hamburger, chips, and cola. People have almost unlimited wants, but limited resources; when wants are supported by buying power, they become ***demands.***

Exchange is the core concept of marketing. ***Exchange*** is the act of obtaining a desired object from someone by offering something in return. For an exchange to take place, certain conditions must exist: for example, (*a*) two or more individuals, groups or companies must participate, (*b*) each party must possess something of value that the other party desires, (*c*) each party must be willing to give up its 'something of value' to receive the 'something of value' held by the other party, and (*d*) each party must be able to communicate and deliver.

The concept of exchange leads to the concept of ***market.*** A market is the set of actual and potential buyers of a product or service. These buyers share a particular need or want that can be satisfied through exchange. The size of a market depends therefore on the number of people who show the need, have resources to engage in exchange, and are willing to offer resources in exchange for what they want.

1.2 *The historical development of marketing*

The idea of marketing is a fairly recent one but has been preceded by others, which are contrasted in Table 1.1. The basic idea of marketing as an exchange process has its roots in ancient history, when people began to produce crops or surplus goods, then bartered them for other things they wanted. During the late nineteenth and early twentieth centuries, goods were sufficiently scarce and competition sufficiently underdeveloped for producers not to really need marketing; they could sell whatever they produced. This became known as the ***production era,*** in which a production orientation was adopted.

The production era

During this era it was thought that people would buy anything, provided it was cheap enough. The prevailing attitude among manufacturers was that getting production right was all that mattered. This was a period of mass production. For example, Henry Ford's objective was to perfect the production of the Ford Model T so that its costs could be reduced and more people could afford it. His marketing policy was: 'The customer can have any colour car he wants as long as it is black.' The production concept assumes that consumers are mostly interested in product availability at low prices; its marketing objectives are cheap, efficient production and intensive distribution. This is used when consumers are more interested in obtaining the product than they are in specific features and will buy what is available rather than wait for what they really want. Today companies use this concept in developing countries or in other situations in which the main objective is to expand the market.

With increasing affluence, people are not prepared to accept standardised products, and as markets become more segmented, manufacturers realise that there are many benefits to be gained from providing specialised products.

The sales era

In the period from the mid-1920s to the early 1950s, manufacturers believed that customers needed to be persuaded to buy more of a firm's products. This era was characterised by aggressive sales techniques, which created profit through quick turnover of high volume. The sales era was concerned with the needs of the seller, not with the needs of the buyer. During this period, personal selling and advertising were regarded as the most important promotional activities.

This approach does not consider customer satisfaction. When consumers are induced to buy products they do not want or need, they will not buy them again. They are also likely to communicate any dissatisfaction with the product through negative word of mouth that serves to dissuade potential consumers from making similar purchases. Today the selling concept is typically utilised by marketers of unsought goods (such as life insurance), by political parties 'selling' their candidates to uninterested voters, and by companies that have excess inventory.

The marketing era

It was not really until the 1960s–70s that marketing generally moved from emphasising aggressive selling. Whereas the selling concept focuses on the needs of the *sellers* and on existing products, the marketing concept focuses on the needs of the *buyer*. The selling concept focuses on profits through sales volume; the marketing concept focuses on profits through customer satisfaction. In the 1980s companies began to move from the policy of selling what they could make towards finding out what the customer wants and then making it. Business people began to recognise that customers are intelligent enough to know what they need, can recognise value for money, and will not buy from a firm if they do not get value for money. This is the basis of the **marketing concept**. Customers, therefore, took their place at the centre of a company's activities. In practice the marketing concept means finding out what a particular group of customers' needs and wants are, finding out what price they would be willing to pay, and fitting the company's activities to meeting those needs and wants at the right price. The motivation is to find wants and fill them, rather than to create products and sell them.

Understanding the nature of customers and their needs and wants, however, is only the first step. A company needs to act on that information in order to develop and implement marketing activities that actually deliver something of value to the customer. The means by which such ideas are turned into reality is the **marketing mix** (see section 1.3).

The social marketing concept

The social marketing concept holds that a company should determine the needs, wants and demands of its customers. It should then deliver the desired satisfaction more effectively and efficiently than competitors, in a way that maintains or improves the customer's and society's well-being. This concept is the newest of the marketing outlooks. The social marketing concept calls on marketers to balance three considerations in setting their marketing policies: (1) company profits, (2) customers' wants, and (3) society's interests. This concept need not conflict with the immediate needs of the company's customers. For example, the Body Shop operates a highly successful customer-oriented business while still promising and delivering low environmental impact.

Thus, a restructured definition of the marketing concept calls on marketers to *fulfil the needs of the target audience in ways that improve society as a whole, while fulfilling the objectives of the organisation.* According to the societal marketing concept, fast-food restaurants should develop foods that contain less fat and starch and more nutrients, and marketers should not advertise alcoholic beverages or cigarettes to young people, or use young models or professional athletes in liquor or tobacco advertisements, because celebrities so often serve as role models for the young.

Concept	Focus	Means	Ends
Production	Mass production	Low-priced products	Profits from sales of standardised products
Sales	Existing products	Selling and promoting	Profits from sales volume
Marketing	Customer needs	Integrated marketing	Profits through satisfied customers
Social	Society's long-term well-being	'Green' marketing	Profits through providing for society's welfare

Table 1.1: *The production, sales, marketing and social concepts contrasted*

Relationship marketing

Relationship marketing is defined as 'the development and maintenance of successful relational exchanges through interactive ongoing, two-way connections among customers, organisations, suppliers, and other parties for mutual benefit' (Harrell, 2002). Traditional marketing techniques are usually concerned with attracting new customers and preventing existing ones from being lured away by competition. It focuses on a business's ability to make a series of single sales to a group of potential customers. The more recent theoretical concept of **relationship marketing** focuses on building high levels of customer commitment by offering exceptional service levels over a long timescale, and generating customers' loyalty by treating them as individuals rather than small elements of large markets.

The rationale for building relationships with customers is based on the long-term financial benefits that can accrue. It is based on two economic facts: (i) it is more expensive to obtain a new customer than to retain an existing customer; and (ii) the longer the period of the relationship, the more profitable the relationship becomes.

Many companies have established **relationship marketing** programmes (sometimes called *loyalty programmes)* to encourage usage loyalty and a commitment to their company's products and services. Relationship marketing programmes have been used in a wide variety of product and service categories. Many companies call their relationship programmes a club. Airlines and major hotel chains, in particular, use relationship marketing techniques by awarding points to frequent customers that can be used to obtain additional goods or services from the company. Relationship marketing is helped by **database marketing** which involves tracking consumers' buying habits very closely, and crafting products and messages tailored precisely to people's wants and needs based on this information.

Exchange marketing	Relationship marketing
Importance of single sale	Importance of customer retention
Importance of product features	Importance of customer benefits
Short timescale	Longer timescale
Less emphasis on service	Higher customer service
Quality is concern of production	Quality is concern of all
Competitive commitment	High customer commitment
Persuasive communication	Regular customer communication

Table 1.2: *Differences between traditional and relationship marketing*

In conclusion, marketers strive to initiate exchanges and build relationships; therefore, marketing can be viewed as an activity involved in *getting* and *keeping* customers. It is the marketer's job to use the resources of the entire organisation to create, interpret, and maintain the relationship between the company and the customer.

1.3 *The traditional marketing mix ('four Ps')*

The **marketing mix** is the combination of four major tools of marketing, known as the 'four Ps': *product, price, place,* and *promotion* (see fig. 1.1 and Table 1.3). The four Ps represent a framework that can be used in developing strategies for marketing managers.

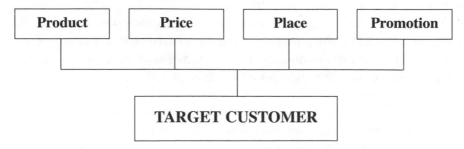

Fig. 1.1: *The elements of the marketing mix*

Faced with a wide choice of product features, prices, distribution methods, and promotional messages, the marketing manager must select and combine ingredients to create a marketing mix that will achieve corporate objectives.

Product

A *product* is anything that can be offered to a market for attention, acquisition, use or consumption and that might satisfy a want or need. It need not be a physical thing but in marketing terms is viewed as a good, a service, or an idea. A *good* is a physical entity that can be touched, for example a car, a camera, or a bar of chocolate. A *service* is an activity or benefit that can be offered for sale, for example a haircut, a concert, or a bus journey. An *idea* is a concept or a policy, for example the importance of parents reading to their children; other marketers of ideas include political parties, churches, and schools.

The product the customer receives in the exchange process is the result of a number of product strategy decisions. Product strategies must take into consideration the other three elements of the marketing mix. (See chapter 7 for further detail on products.)

Price

The amount of money given in exchange for something is its *price*, that is, what is exchanged for the product To a buyer, price is the value placed on what is exchanged.

Marketers must determine the best price for their products. To do so they must ascertain a product's value, or what it is worth to customers in monetary terms. Once the value of a product is established, the marketer knows what price to charge. Because customers' evaluation of a product's worth changes over time, prices are also subject to change. Price may be described in different ways for different exchanges. For example, insurance companies charge a *premium,* a solicitor charges a *fee,* a taxi driver charges a *fare,* and a *toll* may be charged for the use of motorways. Although price may be expressed in a variety of ways, it is important to remember that the purpose of this concept is to quantify and express the value of the items in a market exchange in a way the consumer can understand. (See chapter 8 for further detail on prices.)

Place

Determining how goods reach the customer, how quickly and in what condition involves *place,* or distribution strategy. To satisfy customers, products must be available at the right time and at a convenient place. The marketer has to decide on the structure of **channels of distribution,** from mail-order companies that deal directly with the final customer to long and complex chains that involve goods passing between several intermediaries (wholesalers, retailers, and dealers) before they reach the consumer. A marketing manager may also become involved in establishing and maintaining stock control procedures and developing and managing transport and storage systems. (See chapter 9 for further detail on place.)

Promotion (Marketing Communication)

Promotion is the means by which marketers 'communicate with' both existing and potential customers. The promotional mix is the direct way in which a company attempts to communicate with various target audiences. A company's promotional mix consists of five main elements: sales promotion, direct marketing, advertising, personal selling, and public relations. Promotion can be aimed at increasing public awareness of a company and of new or existing products. (See chapter 10 for further detail on promotion.)

Product	• An Bord Bainne: development of Kerrygold brand for butter • Dairygold: added extra fruit when it relaunched its Sno yoghurt • Lotus Pure Hankies contain 80% less irritant dust than ordinary tissues, ideal for allergy sufferers
Price	• Waterford Crystal: higher price for its hand-cut crystal • Fáilte Ireland: 'Golden Years' breaks for discount prices on accommodation for older people • Ryanair: low-cost flights
Place	• Centra: quick-stop shops • Franciscan Well, Cork: a micro-brewery that sells its product on and off the premises • Dundrum Town Centre: convenient access to the LUAS Balally station and the M50 motorway (southbound)
Promotion	• O'Briens Sandwich Bars: Juicy Bonus Card, get a stamp with every juice/smoothie purchased. Collect 6 for your FREE Juice or Smoothie • Meteor: Choose 5 cent CALLS or FREETEXTS, exclusive to all Meteor Pay As You Go customers.

Table 1.3: *Applications of the elements of the marketing mix by sample companies*

The extended marketing mix for services ('seven Ps')

The extended marketing mix for services is: product, price, place, and promotion, plus an additional three variables or 'Ps', namely: people, physical evidence, and process.

People

The majority of services depend on direct, personal interaction between customers and the company's employees, for example, in a bank, one customer is being served at the desk, other customers are being served at the same time or else are waiting in a queue and employees are providing the service (service providers). These interactions with other people in a service situation may influence a customer's perceptions and expectations of service quality. Service companies such as retailers should, therefore, concentrate on providing a good level of customer service by recruiting the right staff, investing in staff training, and delegating some level of authority to the front-line staff.

Physical evidence

The design of an appropriate physical environment is essential for the delivery of a service so as to compensate for its intangible nature. Physical evidence includes: uniforms, reception areas, appearance of buildings, signage, forms, furniture, equipment, brochures, lighting, landscaping, printed materials, and any other visible cues. These provide tangible evidence of an organisation's service style and quality. For example, uniforms are a way of reassuring the customer of the roles and skills of the service providers.

Process

This refers to a particular method of operations or series of actions, usually involving steps that need to occur in a defined sequence. Poorly designed processes will result in customer dissatisfaction because of slow and ineffective service delivery. Services, therefore, need to be easily accessible and conveniently presented. Clear and easy procedures can help to make the service more efficient.

1.4 *The marketing environment*

The **marketing environment** consists of forces that directly or indirectly influence a company's ability to develop and maintain successful transactions with target customers. The marketing environment consists of a **macro-environment** and a **micro-environment.** The macro-environment consists of the larger social forces that affect all micro-environments and are generally outside the control of the company. The micro-environment consists of the forces close to the company that affect its ability to serve its customers. Table 1.4 illustrates the marketing environment.

Macro-environment	Micro-environment
• sociocultural	• company
• technology	• suppliers
• economic	• customers
• politics and law	• marketing intermediaries
• natural	• publics

Table 1.4: *The marketing environment*

The company's macro-environment

Sociocultural environment

The sociocultural environment can be further divided into (*a*) demographics, (*b*) culture, (*c*) attitudes, and (*d*) current issues. **Demography** is the study of human population according to size, density, location, age, gender, nationality, and occupation. **Cultural forces** affect society's basic values, perceptions, preferences, and behaviour. The sociocultural environment also looks at the way in which consumers' attitudes and opinions are formed and how they evolve. **Current issues** include a large increase in the number of foreign nationals living in Ireland, which has seen the introduction of a variety of speciality products and shops to cater for these needs, for example Polish food and drink. The sociocultural environment is of particular concern to marketers, as it has a direct effect on their understanding of customers and what their needs and wants are.

Technological environment

The technological environment consists of forces that create new technologies, and so create new product and market opportunities. Computer technology has had a profound effect on marketing activities, for example, it helps to make warehouse management more efficient, and therefore less expensive. Computer technology has aided product design, quality control, the production of advertising and other promotional material, and the management and analysis of customer information.

Economic environment

The economic environment influences the decisions and activities of marketers and customers. When an economic outlook remains prosperous, customers are generally willing to buy. Marketers take advantage of this forecast and often expand their markets to take advantage of the increased buying power. On the other hand, if there is a period of recession, during which unemployment rises, customers' ability and willingness to buy many kinds of products decline.

The introduction of the euro currency in January 2002 has had advantages and disadvantages for Irish companies and consumers. It opened up a market comprising 300 million people, reduced trade barriers, and allowed customers to compare prices more easily. Immediately after its introduction, however, higher prices have been reported, especially in the service sector.

Political and legal environment

The political and legal environment consists of forces controlled by laws enforced by governments and local authorities. The political and legal environment is influenced by sociocultural factors, pressure groups, the media, and public opinion. Marketers need to know about the main laws protecting competition, customers, and society. International marketers should also be aware of regional, national and local regulations that affect their international marketing activities.

EU regulations adopted by the Irish government in 2002 have meant that direct marketing companies have had to pull back on the use of telephone subscriber information. The directive means that any 'unauthorised' listening, tapping, storage, and other surveillance of communications is illegal. In addition, the directive states that individuals are entitled to be omitted from printed or electronic directories free of charge.

Natural environment

The natural environment involves natural resources that are needed as inputs by marketers or are affected by marketing activities. Ecological and geographical factors have come to the forefront of marketing strategies over the past ten years. The increasing scarcity of raw materials, the problem of disposing of waste materials and the difficulty in finding appropriate sites for industrial complexes (particularly those with a significant environmental impact) are all factors that are seriously affecting the marketer.

All kinds of external effects of production and consumption have gradually become visible in the environment. River and sea water has become unsuitable for swimming; forests suffer from acid rain and beaches are polluted with oil. On the positive side, a number of companies participate in the application of environmental innovations to production processes. Examples of environment-friendly behaviour include buying free-range eggs, phosphate-free detergents, lead-free and water-based paints.

The company's micro-environment

The company

In making marketing plans, marketers take other departments of the company into consideration, including the top management, finance, research and development, purchasing, and manufacturing. All these interconnected groups form part of the micro-environment. Under the marketing concept, all these departments must 'think customer,' and they should work together to provide superior customer value and satisfaction.

Suppliers

Suppliers are firms and individuals that provide the resources needed by the company and its competitors to produce goods and services. The marketer must monitor the availability of supplies, the price of their supply costs, and their terms for supplying resources. Losing an important supplier can mean that production flow is interrupted, or that a lower quality or more expensive substitute has to be made.

Customers

Customers are vital for the success of a company. Marketers need to be able to find customers, to establish what they want, and then communicate their messages to them. Marketers aim to deliver the right product at the right time at the right price and in the right place and to follow up to ensure that customers are satisfied.

Marketing intermediaries

Marketing intermediaries are firms that help a company to promote, sell and distribute its goods. They include *retailers, physical distribution firms,* and *market research firms.* Physical distribution firms—for example warehouse and transport firms—enable companies to stock and move goods from their point of origin to their destination. The marketer must decide on the best way to store and deliver goods, considering such factors as cost, delivery, speed, and safety. (See chapter 9 for further detail on distribution.)

Competitors

Customers will make comparisons between different products, and will listen to messages from competitors. The marketing manager has to both monitor what competitors are doing now and try to anticipate what they will do in the future in order to position their own products strongly against competitors' products in the minds of customers. (See chapter 4 for further details.)

Public

Finally, some of a company's public form part of the micro-environment. A *public* is any group, including employees, that has actual or potential impact or interest in a company. A range of publics can include *financial publics,* for example banks, insurance companies, and shareholders. *Local publics* consist mainly of a company's neighbours. Local people and organisations may put pressure on the company to take local action, for example to clean up pollution or to sponsor local charities. *Media publics* include newspapers, magazines and radio and television stations that carry news, features, and opinion.

Important terms and concepts

marketing: p. 1
promotion: p. 1
needs: p. 1
wants: p. 1
demands: p. 2
exchange: p. 2
market: p. 2
production era: p. 2
sales era: p. 3
marketing era: p. 3
marketing concept: p. 3
marketing mix: p. 4
social marketing concept: p. 4
relationship marketing: p. 5
database marketing: p. 6
product: p. 7
good: p. 7
service: p. 7
idea: p. 7
price: p. 7
place: p. 7

extended marketing mix: p. 8
marketing environment: p. 9
macro-environment: p. 9
micro-environment: p. 9
sociocultural environment: p. 10
demography: p. 10
technological environment: p. 10
economic environment: p. 10
political and legal environment: p. 11
natural environment: p. 11
company: p. 12
suppliers: p. 12
customers: p. 12
marketing intermediaries: p. 12
physical distribution firms: p. 12
competitors: p. 12
public: p. 13
financial public: p. 13
local public: p. 13
media public: p. 13

Case Study: Sponsorship and the marketing mix: Ford

Ford is a global firm that makes cars and commercial vehicles. It has been the leading car seller in terms of UK car sales for over 28 years. It is based in the US but operates all over the world. In Europe it has 35 sites in 9 countries. Ford brands include Fiesta, Ka, Focus, Jaguar and Mondeo.

One of Ford's successful marketing strategies is the use of sponsorship. A strategy is a set of plans designed to help a business reach its aims. Sponsorship enables Ford to enhance brand value by associating its name with high-profile events. Ford is an official sponsor of the UEFA Champions League. This helps it to reach target customers all over Europe for 9 months of the year. As an official sponsor, Ford has bought the right to marketing opportunities that help to give it a competitive advantage. Sponsorship is just one part of a marketing strategy. The main parts of the marketing mix are defined as product, price, place and promotion.

Product

Ford's products are cars and commercial vehicles. Each different vehicle is targeted at a certain part of the market. Each will appeal to a certain market segment. Ford knows, through its market research, that target customers are also interested in football. It can therefore target the groups accurately. The UEFA sponsorship lets Ford use many communication channels to reach these groups.

Price

Ford products are priced to take production costs into account, allow a margin for profit and to compete with other products from other suppliers. Ford has three aims when it prices its products:

- Cover costs
- Make a profit
- Compete with other firms.

UEFA sponsorship also allows it to compete without using price – this is called non-price competition. In particular, it can build the prestige of its brand. Ford also produces a range of Champions League special edition cars. These are more attractive to some buyers and can have special features.

Place

This refers to where the cars are sold. The football sponsorship allows Ford to spread the brand message around the globe. The Ford dealership network is the largest in Europe. Dealerships are strategically planned for maximum coverage.

Promotion

Promotion is often split into 'above-the-line' and 'below-the line'. The first is paid for directly. For companies like Ford, the main above-the-line promotion has been television, but, new technology and multiple channels mean that traditional communications are becoming less powerful. The UEFA sponsorship combines both types of promotion and helps Ford to cover all of Europe. Advertisements are shown before and after the game, and at half-time. Ford also uses the slot at either side of television breaks to show specific brand messages. These are targeted at the football audience it knows is watching.

In summary, the UEFA sponsorship is a good way for Ford to reach its target audience. It feeds into all parts of the marketing mix.

Source: http://thetimes100.co.uk/studies

Case Study: Creating the right marketing mix: Motorola

Motorola is a company known around the world for mobile, wireless and broadband communications. Its vision is of 'seamless mobility', helping users to get and stay connected to the people, information and entertainment they want. To do this it must first find out what its customers want, and then provide it. It does this through market research, and then by creating an effective marketing mix – a combination of product, price, place and promotion – the '4 Ps'.

Product

Creating the right product is an essential first step in a successful marketing mix. Motorola's main products are:
- Mobile phones, which may allow users to share and listen to music, as well as the usual functions.
- Broadband Internet services, including cable TV and video phones.
- Networking equipment allowing various technologies to interlink wirelessly.
- Communications and information solutions to business and government.

Its most familiar products are mobile phones. Motorola produces phones that are attractive, well designed, easy to use and have the additional features that customers want. These include music players, video and picture features and Internet access. Certain parts of the market have particular requirements, so Motorola caters for them. The RAZR V3i, for example, is ultra thin, has a built-in still and video camera and state-of-the-art speaker sound.

Price

It is important to set prices at the correct level if customers are to be persuaded to buy. Prices will be linked to the product life cycle – in the earliest 'launch' phase, prices will be high to account for development costs. Later, as sales are increasing, costs are reduced so prices can come down. Products that are technologically advanced may be sold at premium, high prices to reflect the initial research and development that has gone into them.

Place

This means how the product actually gets to the customer and refers both to the place where it is sold, and how it gets to the place. Distribution is the process of moving goods from manufacturer to retailer or customer. Motorola distributes through independent retailers such as Carphone Warehouse, network provider retail stores such as O2, Meteor, Vodafone, and 3G and online, via their website.

Promotion

Promotion refers to the ways that a business communicates the existence and nature of its products to its markets. The type of promotion is linked to product life cycle. For a new product, for example, it is important to inform customers of its features.

In summary, Motorola has found out that what people want is to be able to communicate, and to access information and entertainment, on the move. It has put together a successful marketing mix to ensure that customers get what they want.

Source: http://www.thetimes100.co.uk/studies

Questions for review

1. What essential concepts should a definition of marketing include?
2. Explain what is meant by the description of marketing as an 'exchange process'.
3. Trace the historical development of the marketing concept.
4. Briefly explain what the 'four Ps' of the marketing mix refer to.
5. List the main elements in a company's macro-environment that can influence how the company operates.
6. What are the main elements in a company's micro-environment that can influence how the company operates?
7. Marketing is a process that provides needed direction for production and helps make sure that the right products are produced and find their way to consumers. Discuss whether or not this is a good description of marketing.
8. Compare and contrast the sales concept and the marketing concept.
9. What does the term 'extended marketing mix for services' refer to?

2
CONSUMER AND ORGANISATIONAL BUYING BEHAVIOUR

Chapter objectives

After reading this chapter you should be able to
- define consumer buying behaviour
- recognise the stages of the consumer buying decision process
- understand how decision-making processes differ between consumer and organisational buying situations
- understand the influences that affect consumers' buying behaviour
- explain impulse purchases.

2.1 *Consumer buying behaviour defined*

While it is relatively simple for a company to work out who is buying what, from where, and when or how much they buy, the reasons *why* people buy are usually far less clear. It is not always obvious why people respond in the ways they do to the products that are available to them, or how they make the choices they are confronted with. By studying buyer behaviour marketers aim to find out how people make their buying decisions and identify the factors that influence those decisions.

'Consumer buying behaviour' is defined as the study of the buying units and the exchange processes involved in acquiring, consuming and disposing of goods, services, experiences, and ideas (Mowen, 1995). Within this simple definition a number of important concepts are introduced, such as the word 'exchange'. A consumer is at one end of an *exchange process* in which resources are transferred between two parties. Notice that the term 'buying units' is used rather than 'consumers'; this is because purchases can be made by either individuals or groups.

The definition of consumer behaviour also reveals that the exchange process involves a series of steps, beginning with acquiring the product (the *acquisition phase*), moving to consumption, and ending with the disposing of the product or service. When investigating the acquisition phase, researchers analyse the factors that influence the product and service choices of consumers. During the *consumption phase* the researcher analyses how a consumer uses a product or service and the experiences the consumer obtains from such use. The investigation of the consumption process is particularly important for service industries, for example restaurants, amusement parks, and concerts, where the consumption experience is the reason for the purchase. The *disposition phase* refers to what consumers do with a product once they have completed their use of it. In addition, it includes the level of satisfaction or dissatisfaction that consumers experience after the purchase of a good or service.

Consumer behaviour, therefore, focuses on how individuals make decisions to spend their available resources (time, money, effort) on consumption-related items. That includes what they buy, why they buy it, when they buy it, where they buy it, how often they buy it, how often they use it, how they evaluate it after the purchase and the impact of such evaluations on future purchases, and how they dispose of it.

The term *buying behaviour* describes two different kinds of buyers: the personal buyer and the organisational buyer. The **personal buyer** buys goods and services for his or her own use, for the use of the household, or as a gift. In each of these contexts, the products are bought for final use by individuals, who are referred to as *end users*. The second category of buyer is the **organisational buyer** which includes profit and not-for-profit businesses, government agencies (local and national) and institutions (e.g. hospitals, prisons, and schools), all of which must buy products, equipment, and services in order to run their organisations.

2.2 *The consumer decision-making process*

The consumer decision-making process can be divided into the following stages: problem recognition, information search, evaluation of alternatives, purchase decision, and post-purchase behaviour, as shown in fig. 2.1.

Stage 1: Problem recognition

The buying process starts with the buyer recognising a problem or a need. The buyer realises that there is a difference between his or her *actual state* and some *desired state*. Being hungry, for example, leads to a drive to find food. Other purchases may be triggered by a problem: for example, if part of a car is faulty, the driver soon becomes aware of the nature of the problem and the kind of purchase that will provide a solution to the problem.

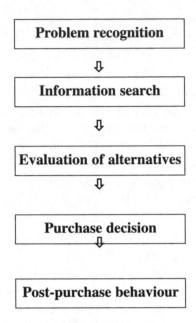

Fig. 2.1: *Stages of the consumer decision-making process*

Stage 2: Information search

The questions to be answered at this stage can include enquiries regarding what kind of purchase will solve the problem, where and how it can be obtained, what information is needed to arrive at a decision, and where that information is available. The consumer can obtain information from several sources, including:

- personal sources—family, friends, neighbours, acquaintances
- commercial sources—salespeople, advertising, dealers, packaging
- public sources—mass media, consumer-rating companies, the internet
- experiential sources—handling, examining, using the product.

Information search can generally be divided into two forms, *internal search* and *external search*. Internal search involves consumers remembering previous experiences and thinking about what they have heard about the product category. The internal search is sufficient, for example, for a consumer who needs to buy biscuits. The consumer will easily remember what his or her favourite brand tastes like, and will also remember where it is on the supermarket shelf. Buying a car, on the other hand, involves external search, which includes shopping around, reading manufacturers' advertisements, and test-driving the car. The purpose of this exercise is to reduce risk. Buying the

wrong brand of biscuits involves very little risk, since the financial commitment is low, but buying the wrong car could prove to be an expensive mistake.
The Internet has had a great impact on pre-purchase search. Rather than
visiting a shop to find out about a product, manufacturers' Websites can
provide consumers with much of the information they need about the products
and services they are considering.

Stage 3: Evaluation of alternatives

This is the stage of the buying decision process at which the consumer uses
information to evaluate alternative brands in a *consideration set*, which is the
group of products that would most closely meet their needs. Having learnt about
several competing brands, the consumer will evaluate the alternatives according
to the information collected or remembered. Certain basic concepts help to explain
consumer evaluation processes: for example, a consumer will typically have a
clear idea of the acceptable price range for the product. The consumer is trying to
satisfy some need and is looking for certain *benefits* that can be acquired by
buying a product or service. Each consumer sees a product as a bundle of *product
attributes*, with varying capacities for delivering these benefits and satisfying the
need. For mobile phones, product attributes might include keypad, camera,
memory card, bluetooth, interface, MP3 player, USB, and price. Consumers will
differ on the priority of these attributes they consider relevant and will pay most
attention to those attributes connected with satisfying their needs.

Stage 4: Purchase decision

This is the fourth stage of the buying decision process, in which the consumer
actually buys the product. The consumer will find the required brand, choose
a retailer he or she has most faith in, and also select an appropriate payment
method. Purchase intention is also influenced by *unexpected situational
factors*. These include in-store promotions (for example eye-catching posters
for other brands) and unexpected information.

A consumer's decision to change, postpone or avoid a purchase decision is
influenced by *perceived risk*. Many purchases involve some risk-taking. The
amount of perceived risk varies with the amount of money at stake, the amount
of purchase uncertainty, and the amount of consumer self-confidence. A
consumer can take certain actions to reduce risk, such as avoiding purchase
decisions, gathering more information, or looking for national brand names
and products with guarantees.

Stage 5: Post-purchase behaviour

Post-purchase behaviour is the final stage in the consumer decision-making process. After buying the product, the consumer will be satisfied or dissatisfied. Post-purchase behaviour usually involves a comparison between what the consumer was expecting to receive and what was actually received. If the product falls short of expectations, the evaluation leads to *post-purchase dissonance* or *post-purchase conflict*. Whether a consumer is satisfied or dissatisfied with a purchase is determined by the relationship between the expectations and the product's perceived performance. Consumers base their expectations on messages they receive from sellers, friends, and other information sources. If the product meets expectations, the consumer is satisfied. If the product exceeds expectations, the consumer is very happy. The most effective way of reducing post-purchase dissonance is to provide a product that meets the consumer's expectations. A failure to solve problems raised by post-purchase dissonance will ultimately lead to irreparable damage to a company's reputation.

The consumer decision-making process, as described above, can involve all or some of the five stages of purchasing. In more routine purchases, however, consumers skip or reverse some stages.

2.3 *Types of consumer involvement in different buying situations*

The level of a consumer's *involvement* is influenced by the perceived personal importance and interest in a buying decision. Personal importance increases as the perceived risk of purchasing increases. *Low involvement* occurs in the purchase of a low-risk, routine purchase, for example toothpaste or milk. In contrast, *high involvement* occurs where an item is expensive, can have serious social consequences, or could reflect on one's social image. When a consumer's involvement level increases, they begin to process information about the product in more depth. This means that they are more likely to think about a purchase decision under such circumstances. As the product or service under consideration becomes more expensive, socially visible, and risky to purchase, a consumer's involvement in the purchase is likely to increase. The involvement concept is important for marketers in order to understand consumer behaviour. The level of involvement influences the amount of information processing and attitude formation and change before a consumer buys a product. Fig. 2.2 illustrates the decision-making process for high-involvement and low-involvement products.

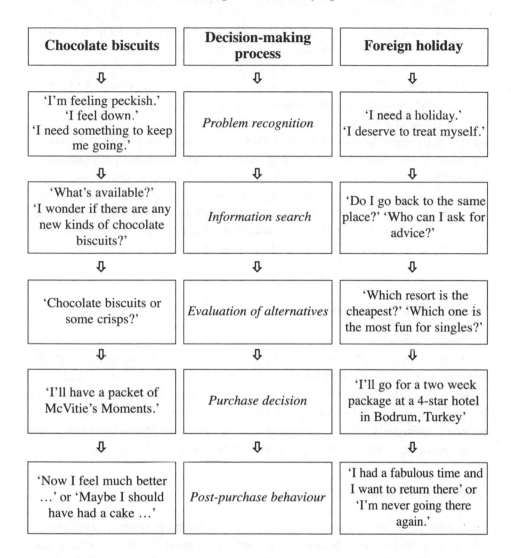

Chocolate biscuits	Decision-making process	Foreign holiday
⇩	⇩	⇩
'I'm feeling peckish.' 'I feel down.' 'I need something to keep me going.'	*Problem recognition*	'I need a holiday.' 'I deserve to treat myself.'
⇩	⇩	⇩
'What's available?' 'I wonder if there are any new kinds of chocolate biscuits?'	*Information search*	'Do I go back to the same place?' 'Who can I ask for advice?'
⇩	⇩	⇩
'Chocolate biscuits or some crisps?'	*Evaluation of alternatives*	'Which resort is the cheapest?' 'Which one is the most fun for singles?'
⇩	⇩	⇩
'I'll have a packet of McVitie's Moments.'	*Purchase decision*	'I'll go for a two week package at a 4-star hotel in Bodrum, Turkey'
⇩	⇩	⇩
'Now I feel much better …' or 'Maybe I should have had a cake …'	*Post-purchase behaviour*	'I had a fabulous time and I want to return there' or 'I'm never going there again.'

Fig. 2.2: *The decision-making process for chocolate biscuits (low involvement) versus a foreign holiday (high involvement)*

Impulse purchases

An *impulse purchase* has been defined as a 'buying action undertaken without a problem having been previously recognised or a buying intention formed prior to entering the store' (Langer and Imba, 1980). Impulse purchases, therefore, are made with no planning. An impulse purchase may be described as a choice made on the spur of the moment based upon the development of a strong positive feeling regarding an object. The visual stimulus of seeing a product available on a shelf is what prompts a person to buy. The motivation is sudden and instant, and consequently such purchases can lead to feelings of guilt.

Various studies have found that as many as 39% of department store purchases and 67% of grocery store purchases may be unplanned (Mowen, 1995). After the purchase has been made, consumers may realise that they have little need for the product and may regret the failure to evaluate more carefully (though this may not deter them from making a similar purchase in the future). The powerful urge to buy seems to override conscious rationality. Marketers have long recognised the potential for impulse purchase of non-essential items such as confectionery and magazines at supermarket check-outs. Faced with a short wait in a queue, shoppers are ideally placed to pick up the visual stimuli from such items, which are unlikely to have been on their shopping lists and would otherwise have been passed by in the aisles.

Addictive Consumption

Consumer addiction is a physiological and/or psychological dependency on products or services. While most people equate addiction with drugs, virtually any product or service can be seen as relieving some problem or satisfying some need to the point where reliance on it becomes extreme. Indeed, some psychologists are even raising concerns about 'Internet addiction' where people (particularly college students) become obsessed by on-line chat rooms to the point that their 'virtual' lives take priority over their real ones.

Compulsive Consumption

For some consumers, the expression 'born to shop' is taken quite literally. These consumers shop because they are compelled to do so, rather than because shopping is a pleasurable or functional task. *Compulsive consumption* refers to repetitive shopping, often excessive, as an antidote to tension, anxiety, depression, or boredom. 'Shopaholics' turn to shopping much the same way as addicted people turn to drugs or alcohol.

Compulsive consumption is different from impulse buying. The impulse to buy a specific item is temporary, and it centres on a specific product at a particular moment. In contrast, compulsive buying is an enduring behaviour that centres on the process of buying, not on the purchases themselves.

2.4 *Influences on the buying decision*

The main influences on the buying decision are
- personal factors
- psychological factors
- social factors.

The ***personal factors*** that influence buying decisions include individual characteristics such as age, gender, nationality, occupation, income, and life-style. People change the choice of goods and services they buy over their lifetime. For instance, their taste in clothes, music and leisure activities are age-related. Many needs are age-dependent, for example baby food. ***Life-style*** covers not only demographic characteristics but also attitudes to life, beliefs and aspirations, hobbies, sports interests, and opinions. A person's occupation and economic situation will also affect product choice: for example, a managing director will buy expensive clothes for work, whereas a factory worker will buy utility clothing and utility shoes.

Psychological factors that influence buying decisions include perception, attitude, learning, motivation, and personality. ***Perception*** is the process by which people analyse, select, organise and interpret information in order to make sense of it. No two people will interpret the same information in the same way, whether it is a product's package or its taste or smell. Perception is of interest to marketers because of the influence it can have on consumer's decision-making generally and on the way it can affect the understanding of marketing communication. Consumers are very selective regarding their environmental perceptions. A person may look at some things, ignore others, and turn away from other things. Because the brain's capacity to process information is limited, consumers are very selective about what they pay attention to. ***Perceptual selectivity*** means that people attend to only a small portion of things to which they are exposed. They pick and choose among items so as to avoid being overwhelmed by advertising clutter.

This over-abundance of advertising illustrates two important aspects of perceptual selectivity as they relate to consumer behaviour: exposure and attention. ***Exposure*** is the degree to which people notice a stimulus. A ***stimulus*** is anything that has an input to any of the senses: examples include products, packets, brand names, and advertisements. ***Selective exposure*** occurs when consumers actively seek out messages that they find pleasant while they actively avoid painful or threatening messages. The smoker therefore avoids articles that point out the link between cigarette-smoking and cancer. Consumers also selectively expose themselves to advertisements that reassure them of the wisdom of their purchasing decisions.

Attention is the degree to which consumers concentrate on stimuli that meet their needs or interests. This can register minimal awareness of stimuli that are irrelevant to their needs. Consumers are therefore likely to notice advertisements for products that would satisfy their needs and for shops in which they shop and to disregard advertisements in which they have no interest. A vivid packet, for example, is one way of actively gaining attention.

Attitude is a person's favourable or unfavourable feelings and tendencies towards a product or service. Attitudes are learnt, which means that attitudes relevant to purchasing behaviour are formed as a result of direct experience with the product, information acquired from others, or promotions. Another characteristic of attitudes is that they are relatively consistent, as they tend to endure over time, but they are often difficult to change. Consumers' attitudes to products can be complex. They can develop attitudes to any kind of product or service, or indeed to any aspect of the marketing mix, and these attitudes will affect behaviour. Changing consumers' attitudes is an important strategy consideration for marketers who are not market leaders.

Social factors also influence consumers' behaviour, for example *peer groups, family,* and *status*. Peer groups will exert a particular type of behaviour and put pressure on the person to conform. Research has shown, for example, that smokers begin to smoke as a result of pressure from their friends when they are young teenagers. The desire to be a fully accepted member of the group is far stronger than any health warnings. Peer pressure contributes to buying for materialistic or social reasons, for example keeping up with social pressure or not to seem to be the odd one out.

Family members can also have a strong influence on buyers' behaviour. Different family members frequently take over the role of buyer for specific product categories: for example, older children may decide on food, choosing environmentally responsible alternatives. Another reason for the family's importance is its role as a *socialisation agent*. Socialisation may be defined as *the process by which people acquire knowledge and skills that enable them to participate as members of society*. Examples of socialisation agents include parents, brothers and sisters, teachers, and the media. *Status* is the general esteem given to a role by society. People sometimes choose products for their social status. A motivation for the purchase and display of such products is not to enjoy them but to let others know that one can afford them. Status-seeking is a significant source of motivation to buy appropriate products and services that the user hopes will inform others of his or her raised status.

In summary, understanding consumers' needs and the buying process is the foundation of successful marketing. By understanding how buyers go through problem recognition, information search, evaluation of alternatives, the purchase decision and post-purchase behaviour, the marketer can pick up many clues for meeting consumers' needs. Consumers' buying behaviour is the result of personal, psychological and social factors, which are useful for the marketer in identifying and understanding the consumers they are trying to influence.

---

1. Consumer analysis should be the foundation of marketing management. It assists managers in:
   a. Designing the marketing mix
   b. Segmenting the marketplace
   c. Positioning and differentiating products
   d. Performing environmental analysis
   e. Developing market research studies.
2. Consumer behaviour should play an important role in the development of public policy.
3. The study of consumer behaviour will enhance one's own ability to be a more effective consumer.
4. Consumer analysis provides knowledge of human behaviour.
5. The study of consumer behaviour provides three types of information:
   a. A consumer orientation
   b. Facts about human behaviour
   c. Theories to guide the thinking process.

Table 2.1: *Reasons for studying consumer behaviour*

Source: Mowen, 1995.

2.5 *Organisational buying behaviour*

Organisational buyers buy products and services on behalf of the organisations they work for. The needs they are trying to satisfy are the needs of the organisation. They buy components for the products that their organisations assemble; they buy accountancy services to enable their organisation to audit their finances; they buy capital equipment so that their organisations can produce goods and services for sale. A definition of organisational buying is 'The decision-making process by which formal organisations establish the need for purchased products and services, and identify, evaluate, and choose among alternative brands and suppliers' (Kotler and Armstrong, 1995).

There are six key stages in the organisational buying decision-making process:

- **Problem recognition:** Similar to the consumer's 'perception of need', someone in an organisation recognises that a problem may be solved by the acquisition of goods or services. Internally, this may occur due to a new product development, under-capacity or problems with quality control; externally this may occur when a buyer sees a product report in the trade press or is offered a promotional price by a potential new supplier.
- **Product specification:** Often in conjunction with other members of the decision-making unit who have expertise and can give technical advice, the buyer will draw up a general description, and then a precise specification of the nature and quantity of the product required.
- **Supplier search:** The buyer will identify potential suppliers of the specified products, and may ask them to submit proposals or give sales presentations to demonstrate their capabilities and indicate their prices.
- **Supplier selection:** This is commonly done by ranking the desired attributes of potential suppliers in order of importance. The list is likely to include a number of purely functional attributes, such as price, delivery, quality and after-sales service, but may also include less tangible features such as corporate ethics and communication skills. Suppliers chosen will be those who most closely meet the key criteria. In many cases, organisations will choose more than one supplier for products they require on a regular basis, to ensure continuity of supply in case of one supplier's default, and to allow the price and service comparison of different suppliers over a period of time.
- **Ordering:** The placing of an order with a supplier may be a one-off activity, or may take the form of a contract to purchase under agreed terms over a period of time. Usually these terms will include payment terms; while consumers usually pay cash up-front before they receive their products or services, organisations usually set up accounts with their suppliers, receiving goods first and subsequently paying for them within a stipulated time period.
- **Performance evaluation:** Buyers collect information about the performance of their suppliers and use this as an important source of information when a similar product is required again. Sometimes this information is used as part of a system for motivating suppliers to maintain excellent performance levels.

Categories of organisational buyers

There are generally four broad categories of organisational buyers:
- **Industrial producers:** typified by manufacturing companies, consists of all the individuals and organisations acquiring goods and services that enter

into production of other products and services that are sold or supplied to others. Buyers or purchasing managers will usually be professionally trained and qualified, and usually working within a separate purchasing department.

- *Commercial and reseller organisations:* consists of all organisations such as retailers and wholesalers that acquire goods for the purpose of reselling or renting them to others at a profit. While they do not physically alter the products they handle in general, they will seek to add value through service. Their purchase decisions in respect of traded goods will be dominated by commercial criteria such as bought-in-costs and resale price, profitability (= margins). The larger retail organisations with an increasingly dominant position in consumer markets have large bargaining power. In recent years some retail groups such as Marks & Spencer have taken the lead in developing stronger partnership links with preferred suppliers.
- *Government and public sector organisations:* exhibit the most formality in their buying behaviour. Traditionally, their approach to purchasing has been highly conservative and slow-moving, often subject to red tape, committees, and rules and procedures. There are signs, however, that public sector purchasing is now becoming more professional and commercially driven, perhaps in response to the general containment of public sector expenditure almost everywhere.
- *Institutions:* such as colleges, hospitals and voluntary organisations are similar to the public sector in their buying behaviour. Traditionally, purchasing has been a semi-formal activity. Recent external influences and policy changes, such as funding constraints, have made purchasing more professional and competitive.

Organisational buyers differ from consumers by being more formalised in their buying behaviour. Organisational buying differs from consumer buying in the following respects:
- bigger order values, in terms of finance and quantity
- fewer buyers, because there are fewer firms than there are individual consumers
- more people in the decision-making process
- more complex techniques for buying and negotiating
- because the purchases are more complex, organisational buyers may take longer to make their decisions
- buyer and seller are often more dependent on each other, which means the firms may buy each other's products as part of a negotiated deal.

Types of organisational buying situations

The organisational buyer faces a number of decisions when making a purchase. The number of decisions depends on the type of buying situation. According to Robinson et al. (1967), there are three categories of buying situations:

- *Straight rebuy:* In a **straight rebuy**, the buyer reorders something without any modifications. When the buying task is familiar and recurring, routine ordering procedures are used to place orders with acceptable suppliers. Based on previous buying satisfaction, the buyer simply chooses from various suppliers on its list, which makes it very difficult for new suppliers to break in.
- *Modified rebuy:* In a **modified rebuy**, the buyer wants to modify product specifications, prices, terms or suppliers. If buyers become dissatisfied with their routine purchases for any reason, they may decide to consider new suppliers; their objectives may be to get better prices, to change the product specification, to improve the delivery times or simply to review the effectiveness of their routine purchases. This provides an opportunity for new firms to get onto the short-list and current suppliers must reassess what they offer and prepare for the likelihood of further negotiation.
- *New task:* In a **new task**, the company is buying a product or service for the first time. In this situation, all the stages of the decision-making process are likely to be in evidence, though the amount of detail included in the product specification and the lengths to which buyers will go to find the best supplier are still likely to vary according to the value of the product and its importance in the operations of the organisation.

2.6 Collaborators

Buying materials and supplier, hiring an advertising agency, or getting a loan from a bank all require that a company works together with another company. These companies are called *collaborators*. Collaborators help the company run its business without actually being part of the company. They are often specialists who provide specific services or supply raw materials, component parts, or production equipment. Working with collaborators helps companies enhance their flexibility, especially in global marketing activities. Before an organisation decides how much it will work with collaborators, its managers should ascertain the company's core competencies. A *core competency* is a talent in a critical functional activity, such as technical knowledge or a particular business specialisation, that helps provide a company's unique competitive advantage. In other words, core competencies are what an organisation does best.

Important terms and concepts

consumer buying behaviour: p. 18
exchange process: p. 18
buying units: p. 18
acquisition phase: p. 18
consumption phase: p. 19
disposition phase: p. 19
consumer decision-making process:
  p. 19
problem recognition: p. 19
actual state: p. 19
desired state: p. 19
information search: p. 20
personal sources: p. 20
commercial sources: p. 20
public sources: p. 20
experiential sources: p. 20
internal search: p. 20
external search: p. 20
evaluation of alternatives: p. 21
consideration set: p. 21
benefits: p. 21
product attributes: p. 21
purchase decision: p. 21
unexpected situational factors: p. 21
perceived risk: p. 21
post-purchase behaviour: p. 22
post-purchase dissonance: p. 22
low involvement: p. 22
high involvement: p. 22
impulse purchase: p. 23
consumer addiction: p. 24
compulsive consumption: p. 24
influences on buying decision: p. 25

personal factors: p. 25
psychological factors: p. 25
perception: p. 25
perceptual selectivity: p. 25
exposure: p. 25
stimulus: p. 25
selective exposure: p. 25
attention: p. 26
attitude: p. 26
social factors: p. 26
peer groups: p. 26
family members: p. 26
socialisation agent: p. 26
status: p. 26
organisational buying behaviour:
  p. 27
organisational buying decision-
  making process: p. 27
categories of organisational buyers:
  p. 28
industrial producers: p. 28
commercial and reseller
  organisations: p. 29
government and public sector
  organisations: p. 29
institutions: p. 29
types of organisational buying
  situations: p. 30
straight rebuy: p. 30
modified rebuy: p. 30
new task: p. 30
collaborators: p. 30
core competency: p. 30

Case Study: Around the world in 80 years: HB Ice Cream

Since HB was founded in 1926, it has grown from a small local business to a global phenomenon, never losing its intrinsic Irishness along the way. For a country that is not particularly renowned for its sunny climate, Ireland has the third highest consumption of ice cream per capita in Europe – only the Danes and the Finns eat more ice cream than us, where the product is seen more as an everyday dessert. Irish people eat on average nine litres of ice cream per annum, and the market here is now worth approximately €143 million.

For HB, the company that has been meeting the needs of Irish ice cream consumers for 80 years now, the brand is all about fun, tradition and quality. According to the company, one of its competitive advantages is its knowledge of the consumer, which it takes and uses to build markets for the Irish palette. Meeting consumers' needs is a given for any successful business of course, so perhaps the most recent and popular example of HB's ability to do this was its decision to bring back the much-loved Wibbly Wobbly Wonder.

As a business HB is aware of the need to observe market trends and to capitalise on them accordingly. One of the sectors that has seen huge growth in Ireland in recent years is health and well-being, and HB has risen to demand in this market. According to HB, one of the most exciting and innovative products recently launched is *Frusi*. This product is really about a new segment. It is made from three simple ingredients – real fruit pieces, frozen yoghurt and wholegrain cereal. So there are three layers: a fruit layer, a frozen yoghurt and a wholegrain cereal layer. The fruit layer is 100% natural – no artificial colours, flavours, sweeteners or preservatives, and it only has 3g of fat per pot. According to HB, it is really about learning that there is something new in the freezer in the health segment. The health segment is a €6 million market which grew by 13% in 2005.

While Ireland is currently in the grip of a health drive, HB studies show that this clean living often means a strict regime from Monday to Thursday, while the weekend is about letting go and enjoying a more relaxed diet. In HB terms this means a higher uptake on light and diet ice creams during the week, with premium and super premium ice cream satisfying consumers at the weekend.

Indulgence at the weekend ties in with the more recent Irish adage that 'staying in is the new going out', as more and more people choose to socialise at home rather than in the pub. This inspires a multitude of 'sharing' occasions, which HB is adept at catering for with its extensive range of in-home ice cream. New flavours such as Chocolate Therapy are in line with the brand's social mission that it must 'initiate innovative ways to improve the quality of life locally, nationally and internationally'. According to HB, they are the clear market leader and believe that the company's Irishness is hugely important to the brand. HB trades very much on its Irish goodness. The recipe is 80 years old, it is traditional with 100% Irish milk, and produced in Killashandra.

Source: http://www.checkout.ie

Case Study: Impulse buying: walking the Walkers walk

The on-going controversies over obesity – particularly childhood obesity – has created difficulties for businesses who operate in the impulse sector, but according to Glyn Billinghurst, Sales Director, Walkers Ireland, those controversies offer new opportunities for manufacturers. Billinghurst revealed that Walkers intend to focus on reducing the fat content of their crisps. The saturated fat reduction of 30% on standard Walkers crisps will be reduced further to 50%. In addition, sodium has been reduced by up to 10% in snacks. The company says the launch of Potato Heads, which is targeted at children has also been a huge success and the product which is targeted at children has 70% less fat than other crisps and no artificial colouring, flavourings or preservatives.

Billinghurst has responsibility for sales of Walkers in both the Republic and Northern Ireland and even though there is obviously a big population difference, Northern Ireland consumers eat just as much Walkers crisps as we do in the south. Sales of Walkers in Northern Ireland are £25 million, representing a 34% volume share of that market. Republic of Ireland sales are over €30 million – which represents a share of 22%. Billinghurst says that this proves that Walkers are on track to make big gains in market share in the Republic of Ireland, as their current market share is where they were in Northern Ireland five years in. 'We have invested heavily in servicing the markets as separate but still have to be able to pool the tremendous knowledge base and expertise we have in all areas – logistics, sales, marketing and new product development – to benefit the business in the distinct markets. We work closely with our distribution partners Boyne Valley in the Republic to maximise on a wealth of local knowledge'. Walkers are now in the position where they are trying to achieve the same success in the Republic of Ireland that they have had in Northern Ireland. They recently became the largest crisp brand in multiples here and now want to achieve that same level of success in convenience stores and forecourts. And the focus on health and wellness will be a big part of that. Their biggest competitor Tayto have been focusing on health for some time now with their 'honest' range and could be said, in some ways, to be ahead of Walkers on that front. It remains to be seen if Walkers can make up the ground in that 'health and wellness' against their main rival. But, Walkers' plans are fairly straightforward. They intend to consolidate their position within the multiples and hold or increase the market share they already have.

But, as Billinghurst puts it, 'we have a job to do in impulse'. The plan for Walkers is to get their products in many forecourts, convenience stores and high street stores. Those top sellers includes products such as Cheese and Onion, Walkers Prawn cocktail, Doritos, and Sensations (Chilli). By winning the impulse customer over to their key top sellers by emphasising 'health and wellness' themes and holding on to their multiple customers, Walkers hope to show strong sales getting their market share closer to Northern Ireland levels.

Source: http://www.checkout.ie

Questions for review

1. What are the main stages of the consumer buying decision-making process?
2. Why are attitudes difficult to change?
3. Why is post-purchase behaviour important for the consumer?
4. Why is post-purchase behaviour important for the marketer?
5. Review your own decision to choose the course of study you have selected and re-create what took place at each stage of the decision process.
6. Compare the decision-making process a consumer goes through for (*a*) a high-involvement product and (*b*) a low-involvement product.
7. Compare consumer and organisational buying behaviour.
8. Outline the four broad categories of organisational buyers.

3
COMPANY ANALYSIS AND MARKETING PLANNING

Chapter objectives

After reading this chapter you should be able to
- analyse a company's capability
- conduct a SWOT analysis
- discuss Porter's three generic strategies
- describe the marketing planning process
- understand strategic business units
- discuss social responsibility and managerial ethics.

3.1 *The company*

The term *company* refers to the business or organisation in itself. A number of companies make up the industry in which a company operates: for example, Ford, Toyota, Opel, Mazda, Renault, BMW and Mercedes are companies in the car industry. Marketing, though essential, is only one functional activity of a company and must be integrated with other functional areas. In determining the costs of manufacturing a product, for example, marketing relies on information supplied by the manufacturing and accounts departments. Marketers work within the framework of the corporate objectives set by top managers, who are responsible for the company's operations.

Corporate objectives are the stated strategic aims of a company, of where it wants to be. These objectives help to create guidelines for a company's marketing plans and are normally presented in the form of financial, qualitative and policy targets.

Financial targets are to increase market share, sales, profit and return on investment over a set period.

Qualitative targets include such matters as service levels, productivity, innovation, and financial and physical resources.

Policy targets are likely to be contained in a *mission statement*. This represents a vision of where the company is today and where it wants to be in the future. It expresses the core values of a company and is intended to guide the company in its strategic development. A mission statement is a generalised statement of the overriding purpose of a company.

For example, when the Ford Motor Company was founded in 1903, Henry Ford had a clear understanding that cars need not be only for the rich — that the average American family needed economical transportation in the form of a low-priced car. Ford also had the insight to know that he could use product standardisation and assembly-line technology to accomplish this mission.

• To provide student-centred education with a career focus for the benefit of the personal, intellectual and professional development of the student and for the benefit of the whole of society *(Cork Institute of Technology)*.
• Fostering a tree culture in Ireland through action and awareness *(Tree Council of Ireland)*.
• The IAVI (Irish Auctioneers & Valuers Institute) is there to represent the property profession in Ireland. Its role is to serve the interests of its members and the profession generally, as well as to safeguard those of the public, interacting between the groups to the benefit of both *(IAVI)*.

Table 3.1: *Some examples of mission statements*

Corporate strategy

Corporate strategy concerns the allocation of resources within the company to achieve the business direction and scope specified within corporate objectives. Although the marketing department is primarily responsible for responding to perceived marketing opportunities, it cannot act without the involvement of all other areas of the company. Corporate strategy, therefore, helps to control and co-ordinate the different areas of the company, such as finance, marketing, production, research and development etc., to ensure that they are all working towards the same objectives, and that those objectives are consistent with the desired direction of the company as a whole.

3.2 Analysing company capability

Marketing managers need to ensure the successful integration and co-ordination of activities in their company. Managers in companies that are marketing-oriented regularly ask questions fundamental to the success of the company, such as:

- Which markets should we be in?
- Where are we now?
- Where do we want to get to?
- How do we get there?

It is important to analyse a company's present position but also to consider issues for the future, by asking questions such as:
- Who are our existing or potential customers?
- What are their present and future needs?
- How can we satisfy these needs?
- What will our competitors be doing in three or five years' time?
- Can we assume that our current mode of operating will be good enough for the future?

These concerns are strategic, not operational, in that they affect the whole company and provide a framework for subsequent operational decisions. The focus is on the future, aligning the whole company to new opportunities and challenges within a challenging marketing environment.

When analysing a company's capability, a manager needs to measure the degree to which the needs of target customers are satisfied by the company's products or services. A manager also needs to be able to measure the company's market share and to analyse whether it is moving up or down, or holding its position.

Evaluating a company's performance is also necessary for analysing the company's capability. Market share too is an evaluative measure for the manager. A manager also needs to be able to answer such questions as:
- How good is our performance?
- What size is our market share?
- Is quality consistently high?

There are two basic approaches for evaluating performance: sales analysis and marketing cost analysis.

Sales analysis looks at the income generated by a company's activities. A manager can compare the sales achieved against what was forecast for the same period. The manager can also make comparisons with competitors' sales.

Marketing cost analysis looks at the costs of generating income. Costs can be broken down into direct costs, such as sales force salaries, and other costs, such as advertising for specific products and the cost of public relations that cannot be allocated to any particular product range or brand.

When a discrepancy appears between the expected performance and the actual performance, the marketing manager will need to take action. The difference between the two positions can be called the **strategic gap**. The marketing manager needs to determine the reason for the discrepancy, for example if the original plan was reasonable, if competitors seized an opportunity, or if someone was at fault. The answers to these questions need to be related back to the employees concerned in order to develop a plan for correcting the discrepancy. Planning occurs so that the gap may be closed, to enable the company to move from a situation it does not want to a situation that it does want.

3.3 *Situational analysis*

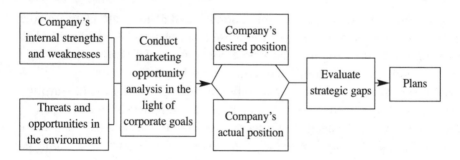

Fig. 3.1: *How situational analysis helps match opportunities to the company*

Situational analysis is the activity of interpreting environmental conditions and changes in order for a company to take advantage of potential opportunities and to ward off problems. Managers need to know the position of their company now if they are to decide where they want it to be in the future. This will involve examining the internal state of the company and examining the external environment in which the company operates. The three essentials of analysis are company, customer, and competitor.

According to Murray and O'Driscoll (1998), when analysing a company's capability it is important to understand

- the company's market position and the strengths and weaknesses of that position
- the feasibility of proposed marketing plans
- the opportunity to build the competence to serve new markets and to outperform new competition.

Managers can use **SWOT analysis** to examine their company's internal and external position. SWOT stands for a company's *strengths, weaknesses, opportunities,* and *threats*. Strengths and weaknesses tend to concentrate on the present and past, and on internal factors, such as the traditional 'four Ps'. Regarding the external environment, however, strengths and weaknesses are usually defined in relation to competitors. Low prices, for example, may be seen as a strength for a company if it is pricing below its nearest competitor but may be seen as a weakness if it has been forced by a price war into charging a low price that it cannot sustain.

Opportunities and threats tend to refer to the present and the future, and take an outward-looking strategic view of likely developments and options. One company, for example, may seize an opportunity to implement new technology, but for another company new technology may be seen as a threat. The SWOT analysis, therefore, helps managers to sort information systematically. If strengths and weaknesses represent where the company is now, and opportunities and threats represent where a company wants to be, then the marketing plan shows managers what they have to do to reach their desired position. The following list is an example of some questions a manager might ask when conducting a SWOT analysis.

Strengths	What are we best at?
	What financial resources have we?
	What specific skills has the work force?
Weaknesses	What are we worst at doing?
	What is our financial position?
	What training does our work force lack?
Opportunities	What new markets might be opening up for us?
	What new technology might be available to us?
	What weaknesses in our competitors can we exploit?
Threats	How will the economic cycle affect us?
	What social changes might threaten us?
	How do our competitors affect us?

Understanding the SWOT analysis

The SWOT analysis, therefore, helps to sort information systematically and to classify it. The scale of opportunities and threats, and the feasibility of the potential courses of action implied by them, can really only be understood in terms of the organisation's strengths and weaknesses. If strengths and weaknesses represent 'where we are now' and opportunities and threats represent 'where we want (or don't want) to be' or 'where we could be', then the gap, representing 'what we have to do to get there' has to be filled by managerial imagination, as justified and formalised in the marketing plan.

3.4 *Establishing strategic business units*

The organisational mission and other strategic corporate goals, once established, provide a framework for determining what organisational structure is most appropriate to the organisation's marketing efforts. For a company that markets only a single product or service, the organisation will be relatively simple. In medium-sized and large organisations that engage in diverse businesses, establishing strategic business units is another aspect of corporate-level planning.

A *strategic business unit (SBU)* is a distinct unit, such as a company, division, department, or product line, of the overall parent organisation with a specific market focus and a manager who has the authority and responsibility for managing all unit functions. AIB Bank, for example, has a commercial division, a trust division and a retail division, which offers traditional banking services for the general public.

SBUs operate as a 'company within a company'. The SBU is organised around a cluster of organisational offerings that share some common element, such as an industry, customer needs, target market or technology. It has control over its own marketing strategy, and its sales revenues may be distinguished from those of other SBUs in the organisation. It can thus be evaluated individually and its performance measured against that of specific external competitors. This evaluation provides the basis for allocating resources.

3.5 *Marketing objectives*

The ability to exploit strengths and opportunities, and to overcome threats and weaknesses, allows the marketing manager to suggest directions for marketing objectives. From the SWOT analysis it should be possible to draw up *marketing objectives* that are consistent with the general corporate objectives and the vision that might be set out in a mission statement.

To be useful, there are two essential requirements for a marketing object-ive. The first is to specify what is to be achieved. The second is to state the time by which the objective is to be achieved. Marketing objectives have to be wide-ranging as well as precise, and they have to link closely with corporate objectives. Marketing objectives revolve around such issues as launching new products, deciding which segments to aim at, or designing new promotional campaigns.

A *marketing strategy* is the means by which a company sets out to achieve its marketing objectives. It defines target markets, what direction needs to be taken and what needs to be done in broad terms to create a competitive position compatible with overall corporate strategy within those markets. It is therefore, concerned with many of the aspects considered in buyer behaviour (Chapter 2). *Strategic decisions* are concerned with the general direction of the company, with where the company wants to be; *tactical decisions* are concerned with how the company is going to get to its desired position.

In general, strategy deals with three areas: distinctive competence, scope, and resource deployment. A *distinctive competence* is something a company does exceptionally well, for example Volvo's emphasis on safety. The *scope* of a strategy specifies the range of markets in which a company will compete. *Resource deployment* is an outline of how a company will distribute its resources between the areas in which it competes.

It is important to distinguish between strategy formulation and strategy implementation. *Strategy formulation* (see fig. 3.2) involves creating or deter mining the strategies of a company, whereas *strategy implementation* involves the methods by which the established strategies are carried out.

Mission
a company's fundamental purpose

⇩

SWOT analysis
to formulate strategies that support the mission

Internal analysis   **External analysis**
weaknesses   opportunities
strengths   threats

⇩

Good strategies
supporting a company's mission
exploiting strengths and opportunities
minimising threats and avoiding weaknesses

Fig. 3.2: *Using SWOT analysis to formulate strategy*

3.6 *Alternative competitive strategies*

Competitive strategy determines how a company chooses to compete within a market, with particular regard to the relative positioning of competitors. Unless a company can create and maintain a competitive advantage, it is unlikely to achieve a strong market position. According to Porter (1980), a company should select a strategy that provides the direction for its operational decisions, which include marketing. Porter has proposed three alternative generic strategies: *overall cost-leadership strategy*, *differentiation strategy*, and *focus strategy*. Each strategy exerts different pressures on companies to ensure that their resources and capabilities are consistent with the requirements of the strategy selected. When choosing a particular strategy, however, it is important to ensure that the chosen strategy will create a *competitive advantage*. This is a company's ability to perform in one or more ways that competitors cannot or will not match. Creating a competitive advantage involves returning to the fundamental marketing questions:

- Who are our existing and potential customers?
- What are their present and future needs?
- How do they judge value?
- When and where can these customers be reached?

Overall cost-leadership strategy

There are a number of ways within a manufacturing environment to reduce and maintain low or lower average unit costs in comparison to competitors. *Economies of scale* suggest that as production volume increases the unit costs decrease. The increased production gives more volume over which to spread fixed costs, thus lowering the average unit cost.

The experience curve is another means of building a low cost base. This concept suggests that as volume increases, so does experience in manufacturing, which might mean less wastage or higher productivity. In other words, the more you do something, the better you become at it. A company implementing overall cost-leadership strategy attempts to gain a competitive advantage by reducing its own costs below the costs of its competitors. This might involve tight cost controls or low-cost production. The emphasis is on cost as a competitive weapon rather than on a range of other factors that customers might find important. Some customers, for example, might be prepared to pay more for added value or a stronger brand image. By keeping costs low, however, a company is able to sell its products at low prices and still make a profit. Ryanair is an example of a company that pursues an overall cost-leadership strategy.

Differentiation strategy

A company implementing a differentiation strategy seeks to distinguish itself from competitors through offering something that its customers value and that is different from its competitors. Differentiation is usually expressed in the form of better performance, better design, or better quality of products or services. Companies that successfully implement a differentiation strategy are able to charge more, because customers are willing to pay more to obtain the perceived extra value. Rolex, for example, pursues a differentiation strategy with its hand-made gold and stainless steel watches. The main advantage of a differentiation strategy is that it takes the emphasis away from price and therefore can charge a higher price. It could also generate buyer loyalty, reducing tendencies towards substitution or switching.

Focus strategy

A company implementing a focus strategy is deliberately selective and concentrates on a narrow group of customers, or a specific regional market, or a particular product line. It proposes to offer a selected item or service by meeting the needs of a clearly defined group far better than any of its more wide-ranging competitors. A focus strategy in itself might not be enough, however, and the company might have to combine it with cost-leadership or differentiation to build competitive advantage. Fisher-Price, for example, uses focus differentiation to sell brightly coloured educational toys to parents of pre-school children. The risk with this segmentation approach is that the segment identified might not be sustainable long term, or might be undermined locally by competition.

Choice of generic strategy

The actual choice of generic strategy depends on three criteria:
- The fit between the demands of the strategy and the capabilities and resources of the company.
- The main competitors' abilities on similar criteria.
- The key criteria for success in the market and their match with the capabilities of the company.

Once these criteria have been assessed, the company can select the best strategy to build a strong position. The company should take into account its potential sources of advantage and how they might best be used to exploit each alternative strategy. These sources of advantage might be:

(i) *skills* – hiring, training and developing key staff who could be in research and development, selling, quality assurance or any area that could help to implement a particular strategy;

(ii) *resources* – both the level and deployment of resources, for example, promotional spend, research and development investment, financial reserves, production facilities and brand strength;

(iii) *relationships* – the quality and long-term stability of supplier-customer relationships provides an asset that is durable in the face of many of the short-term pressures that are created by new entrants and competitors. Such relationships, for example, might tend to favour a focus strategy.

3.7 *The marketing audit*

The marketing audit is a method of reviewing a company's present objectives, strategies, performance, and activities, and its primary purpose is to pick out the company's strengths and weaknesses so that managers can implement improvements. The marketing audit is in effect a 'snapshot' of what is happening now in the company. It should therefore be carried out fairly regularly, within the limits of time and money that can be allocated for the task. The marketing audit was defined by McDonald (1989) as 'the means by which a company can understand how it relates to the environment in which it operates. It is the means by which a company can identify its own strengths and weaknesses as they relate to external opportunities and threats. It is thus a way of helping management to select a position in that environment based on known factors.'

The marketing audit encourages management to think systematically on the environment in which their company operates and on their ability to respond, given the company's actual and planned capabilities. The marketing audit attempts to answer such questions as:

- What is happening in the environment in which we are operating?
- Does the environment pose threats or opportunities?
- What are our relative strengths and weaknesses in handling and exploiting the environment?
- How effective are we in implementing marketing activity?

An effective marketing audit should be:

- Comprehensive
- Systematic
- Independent
- Periodic.

The *external audit* looks at issues such as changes in the socio-cultural, technological, economic and political environments. Competition also has to be analysed very carefully on all aspects of its marketing activities, including its choice of target markets.

The *internal audit* focuses on the effectiveness in achieving the specified objectives of the company. The audit should be undertaken as part of the planning cycle, usually on an annual basis, rather than as a desperate response to a problem. The audit is a systematic attempt to assess the performance of the marketing effort.

3.8 *The marketing and planning process*

The term *strategic marketing process* refers to the entire sequence of managerial and operational activities required to create and sustain effective and efficient marketing strategies. This includes a *strategic marketing plan* and an *operational marketing plan*. The strategic marketing plan guides all planning and activities at the company level, not just in marketing but through-out the company. The operational marketing plan integrates activities, schedules resources, specifies responsibilities, and provides benchmarks for measuring progress.

There are six main stages in the strategic marketing process:

- identifying and evaluating opportunities
- analysing market segments and selecting target markets
- planning a market position and developing a marketing-mix strategy
- preparing a formal marketing plan
- executing the plan
- controlling efforts and evaluating the results.

Stage 1: Identifying and evaluating opportunities

The ever-changing impact of environmental factors presents opportunities and threats to every organisation. Opportunities occur when environmental conditions favour an organisation attaining or improving a competitive advantage. The marketing manager must be able to accurately 'read' the environment and any changes in it and translate the analysis of trends into marketing opportunities.

Situation analysis involves interpreting environmental conditions and changes in light of the organisation's ability to capitalise on potential opportunities and ward off problems. Situation analysis requires both environmental scanning and environmental monitoring. ***Environmental scanning*** includes all information gathering that is designed to detect indications of changes that may be in their initial stages of development. It can be undertaken by the company itself, by professional or industry associations, or by one of the various consulting agencies that specialise in forecasting. The **Internet** is an extremely useful environmental scanning tool. It enables marketers to check out newspapers and their archives, relevant news stories, company press releases, journals, company reports, online magazines, government websites, etc. Diffenbach (1983) outlined some of the benefits of environmental scanning as follows:

- An increased general awareness by management of environmental changes
- Better planning and strategic decision making
- Greater effectiveness in government matters
- Better industry and market analysis
- Better results in foreign business
- Improvements in diversification and resource allocations
- Better energy planning.

Environmental monitoring involves tracking certain variables, such as sales data and population statistics, to observe whether any meaningful trends are emerging. Scanning and monitoring provide information that allows marketers to interpret environmental conditions and to determine the timing and significance of any changes. Situation analysis also requires an inward look at the organisation. The organisation should evaluate its internal strengths and weaknesses in relation to the external environment.

Stage 2: Analysing market segments and selecting target markets

A market is a group of organisations or individuals that are potential customers for the product being offered. There are many types of markets. The most fundamental distinction among them involves the buyer's use of the good or service being purchased. When the buyer is an individual who will use a product to satisfy personal or household needs, the product is being utilised by a consumer. Hence, the good or service is a consumer product sold in the consumer market. When the buyer is an organisation that will use the product to help operate its business, that organisation is buying an organisational product in the organisational market or business market.

Virtually all marketers agree that market segmentation is extremely useful and valuable. Identifying and choosing targets, rather than trying to reach everybody, allows the marketer to tailor marketing mixes to a group's specific needs. An organisation selects a target market because it believes it will have a competitive advantage in that particular segment (see Chapter 6 for further details).

Stage 3: Planning a market position and developing a marketing mix strategy

After a target market has been selected, marketing managers position the brand in that market and then develop a marketing mix to accomplish the positioning objective. A market position, or competitive position, represents how consumers perceive a brand relative to its competition. Each brand appealing to a given market segment has a position in relation to competitors in the buyer's mind. The object of positioning is to determine what distinct position is appropriate for the product. The marketing mix an organisation selects, therefore, depends on the organisation's strategy for positioning its product relative to the competition.

Planning a marketing mix requires a combination of the four Ps: product, price, place (distribution) and promotion. The relative importance of each element may differ for different types of products and different positioning strategies.

Stage 4: Preparing a formal marketing plan

A formal **marketing plan** is a written statement of the marketing objectives and strategies to be followed and the specific courses of action to be taken when (or if) certain future events occur. It outlines the marketing mix, explains who is responsible for managing the specific activities in the plan, and provides a timetable indicating when those activities must be performed.

Stage 5: Executing the plan

Once marketing plans have been developed and approved, they must be executed, or carried out. **Execution**, or implementation, requires organising and co-ordinating people, resources and activities. Staffing, directing, developing and leading subordinates are major activities used to implement plans.

Stage 6: Controlling efforts and evaluating results

The purpose of managerial control is to ensure that planned activities are completely and properly executed. The first aspect of control is to establish acceptable performance standards. Control also requires investigation and evaluation. Investigation involves 'checking up' to determine whether the activities necessary to the execution of the marketing plan are in fact being performed. Actual performance must then be assessed to determine whether organisational objectives have been met. Performance may be evaluated, for example, in terms of the number of sales calls made or new accounts developed. Control activities provide feedback to alert managers because they indicate whether to continue with plans and activities or to change them and take corrective action.

The duration of marketing plans can vary. Plans that cover a year or less are called **short-range plans**; those that cover two to five years are usually called **medium-range plans**; marketing plans that extend beyond five years are generally viewed as **long-range plans**. These plans can cover a period as long as twenty years. Most marketing plans, however, are revised annually, with a detailed three-year perspective, because of the dynamic environment in which companies operate.

A marketing plan serves a number of purposes:
* It helps a company to implement its strategies and achieve its objectives.
* It specifies how resources are to be allocated.
* It heightens awareness of problems, opportunities, and threats.

Companies use many different forms when devising marketing plans, but most plans include the following:
* an executive summary
* marketing objectives
* the present marketing situation
* the marketing mix
* the competitive situation
* personnel deployment strategies for specific tasks
* sales forecasts
* required budgets
* controls and evaluation for monitoring of performance.

In conclusion, analysing a company's capability is an important task for the marketing manager, in conjunction with other departmental managers, which enables them to make more informed decisions about the present and future of the company. As suggested earlier, analysis involves three elements: customer, competitor, and company. (Customer and competitor analyses are dealt with in chapters 2 and 4.)

3.9 *Socially responsible behaviour and managerial ethics*

Society clearly expects marketers to obey the law, but a socially responsible organisation has a responsibility broader than legal responsibility. *Social responsibility* refers to the ethical consequences of a person's or an organisation's acts as they might affect the interest of others (Bennett, 1998). Corporate social responsibility is generally considered to be the 'duty' of an organisation to conduct its activities with due regard to the interest of society as a whole. Baker (1990) defines a social responsibility audit as:

An evaluation or assessment of the policies and practices of an organisation to establish how and to what extent it is behaving in a socially responsible manner, e.g. in terms of employment practices, relationships with its local community, environmental protection, etc.

From this it can be seen that corporate social responsibility covers issues of interest to marketing as well as other business functions. However, anything that affects the way an organisation interacts with its stakeholders could be seen as a marketing issue, for example, **packaging** of goods uses up the raw material, wood, which is used for paper production. As there is a tremendous demand for paper the forests of the world are being depleted. Significant improvements have been taken in the last few years, some firms even using their packaging policies as a selling point. Proctor & Gamble have taken this one step further. Published on their Pampers nappies is the following information: 'Pulp: Made with care for the environment. The traditional chlorine bleaching process is not used. Pampers pulp is purified with an oxidation process. With smaller bags Pampers saves raw materials and energy: less packaging, less waste and fewer lorries for transport'.

Ethics involves values about right and wrong conduct. *Marketing ethics* involves the principles that guide an organisation's conduct and the values it expects to express in certain situations. Ethical principles reflect the cultural values and norms of a society. *Norms* suggest what ought to be done under given circumstances. They indicate approval or disapproval, what is good or bad. Conscientious marketers face many moral dilemmas and the best thing to do is often unclear. Companies, therefore, need to develop corporate marketing ethics policies — broad guidelines that everyone in the organisation must follow. These policies should cover advertising standards, customer service, pricing, product development, distributor relations, and general ethical standards. For example:

- **Products** should be honestly made and described. Commercial pressures may tempt companies to use cheaper raw materials or to use new additives to make the product perform differently. The ethical issue arises when customers are not informed of such changes.
- **Promotions** can involve deceptive or misleading advertising, manipulative sales methods and even bribery in selling situations. Salespeople often face ethical conflicts, for example, either correcting a customer's mistaken belief about a product and thus losing the business, or allowing the customer to continue with the false belief right up to the point of taking delivery of the goods.
- **Pricing** raises ethical issues in the areas of price fixing, for example, pricing below the cost of production in order to bankrupt competitors and not revealing the full cost of purchase.
- **Distribution ethics** involve abuse of power, for example, failure to pay for goods within the specified credit terms. Some stores operate no-quibble, sale-or-return contracts which mean that manufacturers have to accept damaged goods back, even when there is no fault in the manufacture. This has been seen as unethical by some smaller manufacturers who have little negotiating power and few choices of outlet for their products.

Important terms and concepts

Case Study: Tourism Ireland marketing the island of Ireland overseas

Tourism Ireland was established under the framework of the Belfast Agreement of Good Friday, April 1998, to increase tourism to the island of Ireland as a whole. Tourism Ireland seeks to achieve two key goals:

- To increase tourism to the island of Ireland.
- To support Northern Ireland to realise its tourism potential.

This is achieved by working in partnership with industry both at home on the island of Ireland and in the marketplace overseas. Tourism Ireland achieves these goals by:

- Undertaking strategic destination-marketing programmes to stimulate demand for visiting the island of Ireland.
- Facilitating business links by providing promotional opportunities for the Irish trade overseas, e.g. trade shows and joint marketing ventures.
- Acting as an advocate for overseas consumers and trade to influence the quality of the tourism experience on the island of Ireland.

Major changes are taking place in international tourism and travel, driven by social, economic and demographic factors. Customer behaviour is changing, as is the type and duration of holiday-taking, while competition is growing faster than the pool of travellers. The whole process of reaching potential customers and influencing how they choose and buy their holidays is undergoing dramatic change.

Tourism Ireland's 2005 Marketing Plan has responded to changes in the marketplace, but the organisation emphasises that marketing alone cannot provide the solution to growing tourism business to the island. The tourism industry will need to review the tourism product in Ireland in terms of the experience it offers visitors and how the product is packaged so that it offers the most compelling reasons to choose Ireland over competitor destinations.

The tourism industry is constantly evolving and Tourism Ireland has to regularly identify these changes and act accordingly. As a result, it has recognised the following emerging markets and will target these, in addition to existing core markets and best prospects:

- The family market in Britain.
- The luxury segment in Europe.
- Business tourism in all key markets.

Tourism Ireland's marketing plan integrates its efforts in relation to its marketing mix. A good plan can only exist after management undertakes a SWOT analysis. The analysis is important because it enables a business to maximise its ability to compete and identify future opportunities. The tourism industry needs to provide a marketable tourism product that offers potential visitors motivating reasons to visit Ireland. Ultimately, promotion can only do so much. That tourism product needs to develop in light of changing consumer needs, for example by repackaging existing products as part of an experience, by developing new and exciting ranges of products, and by focusing on offering excellent value for money. In summary, tourism is an important source of revenue in Ireland. New trends in the tourism industry provide both opportunities and threats for the sector. Tourism Ireland forecasts and also responds to these threats. It continues to develop and grow overseas tourism business to the island of Ireland.

Source: http://www.business 2000.ie/cases

Case study: Lucozade energy drinks focus on innovative marketing strategies

The sports and energy drinks market has enjoyed unprecedented growth in Ireland in recent years and it is more than a lucrative category for retailers. The sports drinks category is growing at approximately 12% per annum. Combining the theme of health in our society, beverage companies are capitalising on the rise of consumers participating in sporting activities. Energy drinks have always been popular in Ireland, but they more recently carved out a unique niche for themselves amongst the other types of drinks in the soft drinks market. The recent trends seem to be focusing on innovative marketing strategies and new designs for energy products. Growth in the sports drinks market is driven by new brands, brand and flavour extensions and novel product concepts, as well as an increased focus on the role of exercise in health and well-being.

Freshness and consumer friendly packaging will be the main aspects of new products being launched. The sports drink category now encompasses a whole spectrum of different products – from advanced specialist sports nutrition for body builders and serious athletes to lighter products for everyday consumers. The category is now broadening out, with innovation at all levels so as to suit all exercisers, no matter what their age, gender or level of activity. While North America accounted for 49% of sports drink consumption in 2005, and looks set to hold onto its global market lead to 2010, Ireland is increasing its consumption of sports and energy drinks so the market rates should rise in the near future.

Lucozade Energy

A range of exciting marketing initiatives continue to ensure that Ireland's number one energy drink is Lucozade Energy. The addition of a streamlined new 250ml one shot can has been added to the existing product range. The core Lucozade Energy original variant is now also available in this super-sleek new can, which has been specifically designed for fast consumption and delivering energy on the move. Christened Lucozade Energy Charger, the new product's name reflects its energising properties and is complemented by a modern design. The new can is set to capitalise upon current double-digit growth of 13.7% year on year in the carbonates canned drinks sector. The move will also provide yet another boost for Lucozade Energy's leadership status in the buoyant energy drinks sector. In addition, dedicated trade support will drive awareness of the new pack. Research has indicated that this serving portion perfectly matches contemporary consumers' requirements for a revitalising drink they can quickly 'down in one', whilst taking minimum time out during the day.

Lucozade Sport

Backed by the strong brand promise 'better hydration, better exercise', Hydro Active from Lucozade Sport replaces lost fluids fast and provides better hydration for exercise than water alone. Each serving also contains selected energy-releasing B vitamins, vitamin E and 23% of the recommended daily average of calcium – important for good health and an active lifestyle. Two light variants are available – Citrus fruits and Summer fruits – both retailing in a 500ml bottle and containing only 50 calories per serving. To further develop the brand's sports and fitness franchise and status within the sports drink category, Hydro Active will continue to be strongly supported by a heavyweight programme of advertising activity coinciding with the sports calendar throughout the seasons.

Source: http://www.checkout.ie

Questions for review

1. Distinguish between overall cost-leadership strategy, differentiation strategy, and focus strategy.
2. List the factors involved in conducting a SWOT analysis.
3. Why is it important for a marketer to analyse a company's capability?
4. Discuss the stages involved in the strategic marketing process.
5. Give a brief description and an example of (*a*) distinctive competence and (*b*) competitive advantage.
6. List the contents of a typical marketing plan.
7. Write a brief note on the following:
   - SWOT analysis
   - Marketing objectives
   - Mission statements
   - Marketing strategies
   - Marketing audit

4
COMPETITOR ANALYSIS

Chapter objectives

After reading this chapter you should be able to
- identify the various types of competition
- understand the competitive structure of an industry
- outline the steps companies undertake in analysing their competitors
- know the strategies for competitive positions
- assess competitors' strengths and weaknesses.

4.1 *Competitors*

Competitors are other companies that could provide a product or service to satisfy the needs of a specific market. According to Dibb et al. (1997), 'competitors are generally viewed by a business as those firms that market products similar to, or substitutable for, its products aimed at the same target.'

Companies often fail to recognise who their competition is. Sometimes they define 'competition' too narrowly, simply because they define their business too narrowly. For example, if a cinema defines itself solely as being in the cinema business, the management might define its competitors as other cinemas. Alternatively, if a cinema is considered to be part of the broader entertainment business, the management will recognise the competition from video shops, television, night-clubs, the Internet, and restaurants.

In some industries, competition is intense and subject to rapid change. A competitor's strategies or tactics may be the most important factors determining the marketing organisation's success or failure in achieving its objectives. A change in a competitor's marketing mix, such as a change in price, may require an immediate response.

Competition comes from substitutability in goods and services. The term *substitutable* can be interpreted in two ways. Firstly, it can mean that the consumer is choosing among various goods or services — for example, deciding whether to spend money on a new car, or a holiday. Secondly, it can mean that the consumer is choosing a particular product, for example, a new car from among the various manufacturers and price ranges available.

Marketers generally use three terms — product class, product category and brand — to help put the matter of competition into perspective.

Product class is used to identify groups of items that may differ from each other but perform more or less the same function. Any car or beer, for example, can compete against any other member of its product class. Brands of products compete primarily, however within product categories.

Product categories are subsets of product types contained within a product class, for example, beer. There are a number of product categories in that class, including light beer, regular beer, dark beer and imported beer.

To complete their view of competition, marketing managers must consider the matter of brand. *Brands* identify and distinguish one marketer's product from its competitors'. The light beer category, for example, is made up of brands such as Miller Lite, Coors Lite, Bud Light and many others.

There are various *types of competition*, and each company must consider its present and potential competition when designing its marketing strategy.

Types of competition

Perfect competition: This involves many small producers, all supplying identical products that can be directly substituted for each other. No producer has the power to influence or determine price, and the market consists of many small buyers, who similarly cannot influence the market individually. Farm produce, such as vegetables, is often cited as an example of near-perfect competition; the product itself, however, can be differentiated, for example organic and non-organic, or class I and class II quality. Farm produce therefore can be seen to be moving towards monopolistic competition.

Monopolistic competition: Many sellers compete to develop a differential marketing strategy to establish their own market share on a substitutable basis. The idea is that although there are many competitors in the market, each has a product sufficiently differentiated from the rest to create its own monopoly, because to the customer it is unique, or any substitutes are considered to be inferior, for example Maxwell House coffee and Nescafé coffee, or Barry's tea and Lyon's tea.

Oligopoly: A few companies control the majority of industry sales. Each company is large enough to have a big impact on the market and on the behaviour of its competitors, for example Tesco and Dunnes Stores, or Aer Lingus and Ryanair.

Monopoly: Technically a monopoly exists where one supplier has sole control over a market and there is no competition. The lack of competition may be because the monopoly is state-owned, for example Iarnród Éireann, An Post.

4.2 *Competitive structure of an industry*

The performance of a company will be influenced by the structure of the industry in which it operates, because this affects the level of competition in that market. Porter (1980) suggests that there are *five forces* that affect the level of competition (see fig. 4.1). The five forces framework helps identify the sources of competition, in an industry or sector. The framework must not be used just to give a snapshot in time, but, to give an understanding of how these forces can be countered and overcome in the *future*. The five forces are *not independent* of each other. Pressures from one direction can trigger off changes in another dynamic process of shifting sources of competition. For example, potential new entrants finding themselves blocked may find new routes to the market by bypassing traditional distribution channels and selling directly to consumers.

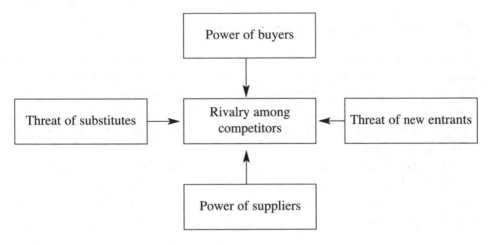

Fig. 4.1: *Porter's 'five forces' model of competition*

The bargaining power of suppliers

Suppliers are in a strong position if a marketer depends on a few powerful suppliers of raw material, and this can lead to high prices and poor product quality. If there is only a small number of suppliers controlling an important ingredient, the suppliers can use their strong position to squeeze profitability in an industry.

The bargaining power of buyers

When buyers possess strong bargaining power they will try to force prices down and set competitors against one another, all at the expense of the sellers' profitability. Buyers' bargaining power grows when they become more concentrated or organised, or when the product is undifferentiated.

The threat of substitute products or services

An industry segment is unattractive when there are actual or potential substitutes for the product. The threat of substitute products or services is often not seen until it is too late. An increase in the number of substitutes can put a ceiling on growth potential and long-term profits. It can also result in problems of excess capacity.

The threat of new entrants

Additional competitors in a market will lead to increased capacity and lower prices. The attractiveness of an industry varies with the height of its entry and exit barriers. A company must consider the possible *barriers to entry* for other companies: these are business practices or conditions that make it difficult for new companies to enter the market. The higher the barriers, the more likely it is that they will deter new entrants.

The most attractive segment is one in which entry barriers are high and exit barriers are low: few firms can enter the industry, and poorly performing firms can easily leave it. Additional competitors in a market will lead to increased capacity and lower prices.

Rivalry among competitors

Competitive pressures among current competitors depend on the rate of growth of the industry. Competitive rivalry is high when there are many competitors of equal size, or where products or services cannot be greatly differentiated. A segment is unattractive if it already contains numerous or aggressive competitors. When market growth is slow, competition is more heated for any possible gains in market share. High fixed costs also create competitive pressures on companies to fill production capacity. Intense rivalry tends to lead to a decrease in profits.

4.3 *Analysing competitors*

The ability to understand competitors and to predict their actions is important to all customer-oriented companies. For a company to be successful in any market, it needs to know its competitors, their strengths and weaknesses, market share, and positioning. Kotler et al. (1999) defines ***competitor analysis*** as 'the process of identifying important competitors; assessing their objectives, strategies, strengths and weaknesses and reaction patterns; and selecting which competitors to attack or avoid.'

To develop an effective marketing strategy, a company must carry out an analysis of its competitors. According to Murray and O'Driscoll (1998), there are seven such steps:
1. Who is the present and potential competition?
2. What is the position they have established in the market?
3. What are their missions and objectives?
4. What is their typical pattern of behaviour?
5. How strong is their resource base?
6. What important competitive advantages do they possess?
7. What are their main competitive vulnerabilities?

Step 1: Identifying competitors

Firstly, a company needs to know who its competitors are. The most obvious competitors are other firms that offer similar or identical products to the same set of customers. Some of these competitors include direct competitors, such as Vodafone, O2, Meteor and 3G; close competitors, such as Coca-Cola and Virgin Cola, and those competitors producing substitute products, such as Pepsi-Cola. Marketers should also clearly identify both existing and potential competitors.

Step 2: Competitors' positioning

Having identified its main competitors, a company must obtain information about the market segments it is pursuing and what product or service benefits it is offering (see chapter 6). This important information will help the company to identify how good or bad the competitors are at serving their customers' needs. They may show potential gaps in the market, or competitive strengths that the company would be unwise to attack.

Step 3: Competitors' mission and objectives

A marketer cannot assume that all competitors want to maximise their profits, and it must therefore act accordingly. Some competitors, for example, may want to maximise their market share. Knowing a competitor's objectives reveals to a marketer what kind of behaviour to expect from the competitor and how it might react to competitive actions, for example a price cut or the introduction of a new product.

Step 4: Pattern of competitive behaviour

The role of the marketer is to estimate competitors' likely actions and reactions. Some competitors react swiftly and strongly to certain actions, while others react slowly. There may be some who react only to certain types of pressures and not to others. At the same time, other competitors can be completely unpredictable. It is best, therefore, to build up a picture of typical behaviour patterns of competitors. This should help the marketer to decide how best to attack competitors, or how best to defend one's own current position.

Step 5: Competitive resource base

At this point the marketer should have a good idea of competitors' position in the market and their likely patterns of reaction. A company must then identify each competitor's resource base, that is, its internal resources. Competitors may call on their financial, marketing, managerial, manufacturing or technological resources when they want to implement strategies and achieve their goals. By analysing their own resources, marketers should receive a clear indication of their strengths and weaknesses.

Step 6: Main advantages and disadvantages

From the previous steps a marketer can identify the main advantages and disadvantages of each competitor. A company can decide how and where to compete according to these findings, for example, it might avoid the areas where its competitors are strongest and attack their weak areas.

4.4 *Direct and indirect competitors*

The most obvious competitors are other organisations which offer similar products or services. Suppliers of substitute products and services, however, highlight the indirect competitors, who must also be analysed. Five levels of competitors can be identified:

Direct competition

Pepsi Cola is a direct competitor to Coca-Cola. Both products offer similar benefits to the same general market. The production methods employed are also very similar, although the actual formula for the basic cola essence is somewhat different in both companies since these products are in direct competition.

Close competition

Is Pepsi a competitor to Club Orange? Both products offer similar benefits to similar consumers. The difference between orange and cola flavour is easier to recognise than the difference between Coca-Cola and Pepsi, but basically the products are substitutes for each other. In any analysis of drinks, all fizzy drinks need to be considered. It could be argued that other fizzy drinks include Ballygowan sparkling mineral water and champagne, but we would be moving away from a strict interpretation of close competition.

Products of a similar nature

Perrier is a naturally sparkling water from Southern France. The water comes up through a field of natural gas, hence the claim to be naturally sparkling as opposed to having added carbon dioxide, which is the case with Pepsi or other sparkling waters. Perrier, however, is targeted at an adult market, rather than the younger age targeted by Pepsi. This makes Perrier less of a close competitor. Champagne also has an alternative way of producing the fizz. 'Methode Champenoise' is a secondary fermentation of the wine after it has been bottled. It is not the different way of producing the bubbles, however, but the positioning of the product that makes it less relevant when considering competitors.

Substitute products

Is ice cream a substitute for a fizzy drink? In some situations this is a reasonable choice. Marketers need to consider those products which can substitute in this way. The study of buyer behaviour is critical in deciding how wide such a study should go.

Indirect competition

Any product that competes for the same buying power could be considered a competitor. There may be indirect competition between a foreign holiday and a new car. Or, for low-value items there could be a choice between a newspaper and a Sprite for a student living on a limited grant.

4.5 *Assessing competitors' strengths and weaknesses*

Marketers need to identify accurately each competitor's strengths and weaknesses. As a first step, a company gathers key data on each competitor's business over the last few years. Companies normally learn about their competitors' strengths and weaknesses through secondary data, personal experience and word of mouth. They can also increase their knowledge by conducting primary marketing research with customers, suppliers and dealers. A growing number of companies have turned to *benchmarking*, comparing the company's products and processes to those of competitors or leading firms in other industries to find ways of improving quality and performance. Benchmarking has become a powerful tool for increasing a company's competitiveness.

According to Kotler et al. (1999), a company can spend too much time and energy tracking competitors. A company can become so competitor-centred that it loses its customer focus, which is even more important. A *competitor-centred company* is one whose moves are based mainly on competitors' actions and reactions. The company spends most of its time tracking competitors' moves and market shares, and trying to find strategies to counter them. The company becomes too reactive, and rather than carrying out its own consistent customer-oriented strategy, it bases its moves on competitors' moves. As a result, it does not move in a planned direction towards achieving its goals. It does not know where it will end up, since so much depends on what the competitors do.

A *customer-centred company*, in contrast, focuses more on customer developments in designing its strategies. The customer-centred company is in a better position to identify new opportunities and set a strategy that makes long-term sense. By watching customer needs evolve, it can decide what customer groups and what emerging needs are the most important to serve, given its resources and objectives.

4.6 *Strategies for competitive position*

The strategy that is appropriate for a company depends on its competitive position in the industry. There are four *types of competitive position* that firms can occupy in a market: market leader, challenger, follower, and nicher.

Market leader

This is the company with the highest market share. It maintains its position by changing prices, introducing new products, increasing distribution, and promotion. The strategies of a market leader include

- expanding the total market – by looking for new uses and new users, and by increasing the use of its products or services
- protecting present market share – through market diversification, continuing to innovate, extending product lines, protecting weak areas, and strategic withdrawal
- expanding market share – by acquiring other businesses.
  Examples: Microsoft; Gillette.

Market challenger

This company is not a market leader and therefore has to fight aggressively for additional market share. Market challengers are organisations with a smaller market share, but who are close enough to pose a serious threat to the leader. However, an aggressive strategy can be costly, if the challenger is thinking of attacking where there is uncertainty over winning. Before making a concerted effort to steal share, therefore, the challenger needs to ask itself whether market share really matters so much, or whether there would be greater benefit from working on getting a good return on investment from existing share. The strategies of a market challenger include

- attacking the market leader or other companies – attacking their strengths, attacking from all directions (multi-prong approach), bypassing the competition and identifying easier markets, guerrilla attacks (annoying competitors with unpredictable attacks).
  Example: Ryanair.

Market follower

This company is in a similar position to the market challenger, except that it prefers to follow rather than attack the leader. Given the resources needed, the threat of retaliation and the uncertainty of winning, many organisations favour a far less aggressive stance, acting as market followers. There are two types of followers. First, there are those who lack the resources to mount a serious challenge and prefer to remain innovative and forward thinking, without disturbing the overall competitive structure in the market by encouraging open warfare. Often, any lead from the market leader is willingly followed. This might mean adopting a 'me too' strategy, thus avoiding direct confrontation and competition.

The second type of follower is the organisation that is simply not capable of challenging and is content just to survive, offering little competitive advantage. Often, smaller car rental firms operate in this category by being prepared to offer a lower price, but not offering the same standard of rental vehicle or even peace of mind should things go wrong. A recession can easily eliminate the weaker members of this category. The strategies of a market follower include

- holding on to present market share and trying to increase it
- using market segmentation
- using R&D efficiently
- maintaining high product quality.
  Examples: Independent radio stations; Dunnes Stores (its own range of breakfast cereals).

Market nicher

Some organisations, often small, specialise in areas of the market that are too small, too costly or too vulnerable for the larger organisation to contemplate. Niching is not exclusively a small organisation strategy, as some larger organisations may have divisions that specialise. The key to niching is the close matching between the needs of the market and the capabilities and strengths of the company. The specialisation offered can relate to product type, customer group, geographic area or any aspect of product/service differentiation. The strategies of a market nicher include

- avoiding competition in order to succeed
- specialising in customer, product or marketing mix lines
- using multiple niching
- finding safe market segments.
  Examples: Caterpillar; Ferrari; Lily O'Briens hand-made chocolates.

4.7 *The competitive triangle*

The competitive triangle (fig. 4.2) shows that customers have choices. From the top of the triangle, customers can evaluate the different product offerings of all companies and their competitors. They will choose to buy products or services from companies that best match their requirements.

As we saw in chapter 2, the consumer buying decision process is complex. Marketers must therefore try to influence consumers in such a way that the products or services of their companies are chosen. In other words, they must endeavour to gain a ***competitive advantage***, that is, something a product or a company has that is desired by consumers and not matched by competitors. In summary, to gain the strongest possible competitive advantage, a company must continuously analyse not just its present and potential customers and the company itself but also all its competitors. To be successful it needs to sustain that competitive advantage over time and to fight off those who would like to have a share of any profitable business that is established. Sustaining a competitive advantage requires the continual collection and use of marketing information to ensure that the needs of the target markets are being met more effectively and efficiently than by the competition and that adjustments to the marketing mix are made if changes in the environment threaten the business.

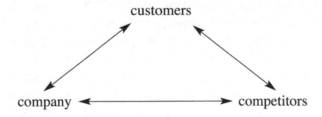

Fig. 4.2: *The competitive triangle*

Important terms and concepts

competitors: p. 55
substitutable: p. 55
product class: p. 56
product categories: p. 56
types of competition: p. 56
perfect competition: p. 56
monopolistic competition: p. 56

oligopoly: p. 56
monopoly: p. 56
competitive structure of an industry:
  p. 57
'five forces' model of competition:
  p. 57
bargaining power of suppliers: p. 57

Case Study: A new strategy for a global leader – Intel®

Intel® is recognised as the world's fifth most valuable brand valued at around $35 billion. Most of the world's personal computers are powered by an Intel microprocessor. Through high levels of investment and concentrating on microprocessors, Intel® was able to leave its competitors behind. It invested billions of dollars in highly productive manufacturing plants that could produce more processors in a day than some of their rivals could produce in a year.

Today Intel® continues to raise the bar. In January 2006 it launched its new strategy based on identifying and creating new markets. Instead of just focusing on desktops Intel® will play a key technological role in a range of fields including healthcare, consumer electronics and wireless communications. Intel® aims to develop integrated packages – platforms – to provide complete solutions to its key customers such as Sony and Philips. Its strategy is to be at the heart of new developments in all areas such as home entertainment, security and medical care that will generate new revenue streams.

Intel® launched its new strategy at the Las Vegas Consumer Electronics Show in January 2006. Part of the new strategy was a new logo redesigned to show that Intel® was moving forward. Intel's communication messages show it is at the leading edge of technology development, creating products before its competitors do.

Its new strategy has a strong focus on finding out what customers want and then providing it. Clear communication is the key to this. The company has been restructured from top to bottom to reflect the emphasis on communication. Intel® also increased its range of end customers to include mobile phone companies and hospitals. The market for high-tech products and systems is broken up into four discrete segments and recognising this Intel® created four sectors representing these segments. These are notebooks, PCs, wireless and software. New product development focuses on particular markets, for example in business Intel® has developed a range of chips for personal organisers, servers and a range of other applications.

Intel® has recognised that the market segment is constantly changing and has therefore developed new strategies to keep itself at the leading edge of the market.

Source: http://www.tt100.biz

Case Study: Dyson cleans up in America

Hoover, invented in 1907 in the United States, was put up for sale in February 2006 by its American parent company as sales of the pioneering vacuum cleaner had dropped to unsupportable levels in the face of stiff competition from the British-designed bagless vacuum cleaner, Dyson.

When Dyson entered the US market in 2002, the American manufacturer had a tight grip on its home market with a 36% share. Yet, the Dyson with its modernist looks and unique engineering has managed to erode Hoover's commanding position in America every year since.

In 2004, Dyson managed to capture almost 14% of the market while Hoover's share slipped to about 20%. In 2005, Hoover's share slipped again to almost 13% and Dyson's sales went beyond the important 20% mark. Hoover's sales had plunged so far on its home turf that it was forced to explore strategic alternatives for the brand, which included the possibility of a sale.

In early 2006, Maytag, Hoover's owners could no longer carry the burden of its underperforming product line and decided to sell its floor care business. On 31 March, 2006, Whirlpool completed its acquisition of Maytag Corporation including its Hoover brand.

Much of Dyson's success in America came after its appearance in the background on hits shows such as *Will and Grace* and *Friends*. According to Dyson's chief executive, Martin McCourt, 'Without R&D and relentless innovation, we wouldn't be able to take on huge markets like the US or stay ahead of competitors. It's our technology that Americans clearly understand and appreciate.'

Source: www.timesonline.co.uk

Questions for review

1. What would a company hope to gain by analysing its competitors?
2. Outline the steps involved in analysing competitors.
3. What questions should a marketing manager attempt to answer when undertaking a competitor analysis?
4. How would a company analyse the competitive structure of an industry?
5. Discuss the various competitive positions in marketing and the appropriate strategies for each position.
6. Discuss direct and indirect competition.

5
MARKETING INFORMATION AND RESEARCH

Chapter objectives

After reading this chapter you should be able to
- recognise the importance of information to a company
- define the marketing information system and its elements
- describe the steps involved in the marketing research process
- understand the applications of marketing research.

5.1 *The importance of information to a company*

'Information is the principal resource used by a marketer, and decisions can only be as good as the information used' (Murray and O'Driscoll, 1998).

To apply the marketing concept, marketers require a constant flow of information on every aspect of marketing. *Data* are simply raw facts and recorded measures of wants, whereas *information* is data in a form suitable for decision-making. The proper collection of data is the cornerstone of any information system. The quality of marketing decisions is usually dependent on the quality of information that informs those decisions. A marketer requires information on a wide range of areas, including defining target markets, the developing of marketing mixes, and the formulating of long-term strategic plans. Better planning, data collection and analysis lead to more reliable and useful findings, and therefore marketers are able to make decisions that are more likely to satisfy the needs and wants of the target market segments.

A company that is prepared to make a marketing decision without first assessing likely market reaction runs a risk of failure. In general, gathering information offers a company a foundation on which it can adjust to the changing environment in which it operates.

5.2 *The marketing information system*

In order to serve the information needs of the organisation and to support decision-making marketers need to focus not only on collecting data and information, but also on how to handle and manage issues of storage, access and dissemination. A research report is no use to anyone if nobody knows where it is or that it exists, or if the people who need it do not have the authority or means to access it. Marketing information, therefore, has become increasingly important. As a result, many firms have designed their own systems for processing the information for use by their marketing managers. A firm needs to co-ordinate the information it collects from a variety of sources (see section 5.3) into a *marketing information system*. 'A marketing information system (MIS) is an organised set of procedures and methods by which pertinent, timely and accurate information is continually gathered, sorted, analysed, evaluated, stored and distributed for use by marketing decision makers' (Zikmund and d'Amico, 1996).

Fig. 5.1 summarises the elements of a marketing information system. An MIS can be one of a number of management information systems used by a firm, but it is mainly used by marketing managers. It provides marketers with timely and comprehensive information to aid their decision-making. Previously, marketing information systems stressed the collection and organisation of marketing data. An MIS now emphasises the need for the system to be easier to use so as to encourage its use by marketing managers, who require ready access to information for their decisions.

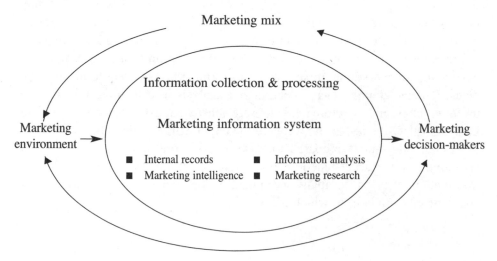

Fig. 5.1: *The marketing information system*

Most marketing information systems use databases and high-powered computers; some use advanced scanning technology for stock control and ordering. For some companies the marketing information system may be a well-organised, formal system, whereas for others it may be much more informal.

The elements of the marketing information system are *internal records, marketing intelligence, information analysis*, and *marketing research*.

Internal records

Internal records comprise information collected from sources within the company, including
- sales records
- accounts data
- production schedules
- purchasing details
- sales representatives' reports
- customer enquiries and complaints
- loyalty card schemes (for example Luigi Malone's Customer Royalty card)
- product returns
- research studies.

Internal records enable a manager to evaluate the company's marketing performance and to discover possible marketing problems and opportunities. Information from internal records is usually faster and cheaper to access than information from other sources, but it also has a number of limitations. Because internal information is usually collected for other purposes, it may be incomplete or in the wrong form for use in making marketing decisions.

Marketing intelligence

Marketing intelligence is everyday information about events in a company's marketing environment that helps managers to prepare and adjust marketing plans. Marketing intelligence involves developing a perspective on information that provides a competitive edge, for example the opening up of a new market segment. The sources of marketing intelligence include
- employees
- customers
- competitors
- suppliers
- intermediaries

- published reports
- advertisements
- trade fairs and conferences
- buying intelligence from research agencies
- the internet, especially the world wide web.

Companies can also buy intelligence information from outside suppliers, such as Dun and Bradstreet, the world's largest research company, which sells data on brand shares, retail prices, and percentages of shops stocking different brands.

Information analysis

Data gathered by a company's marketing information system may require further analysis for transformation into practical, usable information. Sometimes managers experience difficulties in applying the information to its marketing problems and decisions. Computer programs that include regression analysis and correlation may help with these.

Marketing research

This is the systematic gathering, analysing and reporting of significant inform-ation relating to exchanges that take place between a company, or its products and services, and its customers. Tull and Hawkins (1992) defined marketing research as 'a formalised means of obtaining information to be used in making marketing decisions.'

A successful business depends on developing an effective two-way ex-change and communication process with its customers. Research findings are essential to planning and developing marketing strategies. Information on target markets makes a vital contribution to planning the marketing mix and the controlling of marketing activities. This means that when adequate information about customers is available, the marketing concept can be better implemented.

Marketing research, therefore, is a scientific method of finding data on markets, analysing the information, and using it as a basis for decision-making. Market research can enable a company

- to investigate what has been happening in the past in the market
- to understand what is happening at present
- to try to anticipate what will happen in the future.

Marketing research can help a company to gather both **quantitative** and **qualitative information** about its customers. If the research objectives require data to be collected on how many people hold similar views or display particular characteristics, the research is described as being quantitative. Quantitative information lists how many customers and potential customers are accessible, how much they spend on the company's product, and where they spend their money. If the research objectives require information to be generated about how people think and feel about issues, or why they take certain decisions and behave as they do, then the research is described as being qualitative. Qualitative information lists the attitudes, opinions and preferences of customers and suggests why they prefer to buy one company's products rather than those of its competitors.

The need for marketing research sometimes arises because the organisation needs specific details about a target market, which is a well-defined, straightforward descriptive research task. Sometimes, though, the research need arises from a much broader question, such as why a new product is not achieving expected market share.

5.3 *The marketing research process*

Step 1: Define the problem and research objectives

The research process begins with the recognition of a marketing problem or opportunity. Marketing research may be used to evaluate product, promotion, distribution or pricing alternatives. Before research begins, the marketing manager and the researcher should agree on the nature of the marketing problem or opportunity to be investigated: for example, as changes occur in a company's external environment, marketing managers are faced with questions such as 'Should we change the existing marketing mix—and if so, how?'

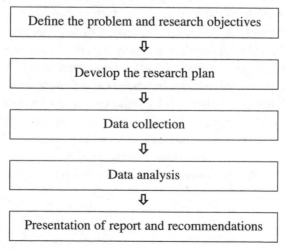

Fig. 5.2: *The marketing research process*

Definition of research objectives

The culmination of the process of problem or opportunity formulation is a statement of the research objectives. These consist of the precise information necessary and desired to solve the marketing problem. Objectives must be specific and limited in number: the fewer the research objectives, the easier it is to keep track of them and to make sure each is considered fully and to determine the most appropriate method. Often researchers state research objectives in the form of a hypothesis. This is a statement about a relationship between two or more variables that can be tested with empirical data. The development of research hypotheses sets the stage for creating the research plan or design.

At this early stage of the research process it is often necessary to conduct *exploratory research*. Exploratory research is usually small-scale research undertaken to define the exact nature of the problem and to gain a better understanding of the environment within which the problem has occurred. Exploratory research tends to be highly flexible, with researchers following ideas, clues, and hunches. Exploratory research is conducted if the nature of a problem or issue is unclear; it is concerned with exploring possibilities rather than finding specific answers. As the researcher moves through the exploratory research process, a list of problems and sub-problems should be developed.

The research objectives may also be answered by using descriptive research or causal research. *Descriptive research* is conducted to answer 'who', 'what', 'when', 'where' and 'how' questions. It is implicit in descriptive research that the management already knows or understands the underlying relationships of the problem area. Descriptive research is used to outline the factors that will influence marketing decisions, such as the market potential for a product, customers' attitudes, and competitors' strategies. An example of descriptive objectives is determining the average frequency of purchase.

In *causal research* the researcher investigates whether one variable causes or determines the value of another variable. A variable is a symbol or concept that can assume any set of values. A *dependent variable* is a variable expected to be predicted or explained; an *independent variable* is a variable in the experiment that the researcher can to some extent manipulate or change. An independent variable is expected to influence the dependent variable. An independent variable in a research project is a presumed cause of the dependent variable, which is the presumed effect. For example, does the level of advertising (independent variable) determine the level of sales (dependent variable)?

Step 2: Develop the research plan

When undertaking a marketing research project, a marketer must be careful not to duplicate research if the required information is already available from another source. A researcher should start by collecting any information that is already available and then develop a plan for collecting, analysing and presenting the information to the client. In preparing the *research plan,* the researcher must identify clearly what additional data are needed, and then establish how to collect that data. This may involve collecting both primary and secondary data. Once the researcher has recognised that new information is needed that is not already available, he or she must decide the best source for that information. *Primary data* consist of original sources of information used for providing the information required for the research objectives. *Secondary data* consist of information that have already been collected for another purpose.

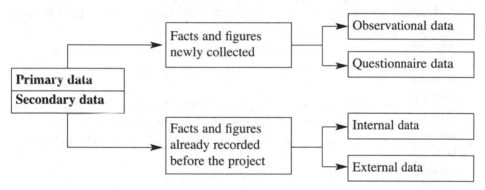

Fig. 5.3: *The differences between primary and secondary data*

There are two types of secondary data: internal and external. *Internal data* are obtained from within the company, for example

- sales statistics
- customer records
- sales representatives' reports
- financial statements
- research reports
- customer lists.

Once the internal sources have been consulted, a researcher should then seek external data. *External data* are obtained from outside the company, for example

- census of population (Central Statistics Office)
- business or trade publications (e.g. *BusinessPlus, Irish Marketing Journal, Factfinder online, Checkout Ireland*)

- government departments (e.g. Enterprise, Trade and Employment, Agriculture and Food)
- universities, institutes of technology, colleges of further education
- state agencies and other official bodies (e.g. An Bord Bia, Enterprise Ireland, FÁS)
- chambers of commerce and European business information centres
- local authorities (city councils and county councils)
- European Institutions (e.g. European Commission, European Parliament, European Foundation for the Improvement of Living and Working Conditions)
- annual reports
- online databases
- online database vendors (e.g. America Online, CompuServe, Dow Jones)
- Internet newsgroups and special-interest groups
- CD-ROM database packages (e.g. US Census Bureau offers TIGER files which map locations of all US streets, airports, etc.)
- company websites, for example, www.esb.ie, www.obriensonline.com, www.peugot.ie, www.irishrail.ie, www.smurfit-group.com)

Researchers generally begin by using secondary data and then continue by using primary data. Secondary data have a number of advantages:
- They save time, as they have already been collected and are readily available.
- They are cost-effective (available free internally).
- They can be used as a source of ideas and a starting point for further primary research.

Secondary data may also have disadvantages, however:
- They may be out of date.
- The data collected for another purpose may not be specific enough for the needs of the researcher.
- There may be doubts about the accuracy of the data, such as errors in the original research design, or the sample may be inappropriate.

Gaps in secondary data can be filled through primary research, for example by *observation*, *survey*, and *experiment*.

1 Observation

Observational research is used to collect information about the behaviour and actions of people or by observing the results of those actions. The data are collected by observing some action or actions of the respondent. Observation is a particularly useful technique in situations where people find it difficult to give verbal accounts of their behaviour, for example identifying the most common route taken through a supermarket. Observational research depends largely on the skills of the observer. It is less expensive than other forms of research, and can be collected by personal or mechanical observation. In **personal observation** a researcher may pose as a customer in a shop and observe customers buying from a particular product category. With **mechanical observation**, companies may use mechanical tools to observe people: for example, supermarket bar-code scanners continually monitor consumers' purchases. The A.C. Nielsen company monitors the viewing habits of television viewers. Tachistoscopes (measuring visual perception) and galvanometers (measuring changes in the electrical resistance of a person's skin) are used to indicate degrees of interest in advertisements.

2 Surveys

Surveying involves the collection of data directly from respondents. It is the most widely used and the most flexible method of gathering primary data. Survey methods include direct personal interviews, telephone questionnaires, and postal questionnaires. The selection of a survey method depends on the nature of the problem, the data needed to test the hypothesis, and the resources available to the researcher.

Personal interviews

Focus groups involve an interviewer (known as a facilitator) chairing a discussion among a group, typically of six to ten people. The facilitator intervenes only to keep the conversation on the right themes, preventing it from wandering from relevant topics. The researcher narrows the conversation during the session, concentrating on a specific brand, product, or advertisement—hence the term 'focus group'. The whole discussion is, ideally, recorded on tape, and preferably on video, to monitor non-verbal behaviour accompanying responses.

Advantages of this method include:

- Focus groups allow interviewers to explore issues with several people at once.
- The effects of group dynamics stimulate members to reveal beliefs and views that may not have been so freely expressed in one-to-one interviews.
- Researchers can ask probing questions to clarify responses.

Disadvantages include:
- If the group includes some dominant people, less assertive people may be discouraged from full participation.
- Focus groups usually employ small sample sizes to keep time and costs down, and it may be misleading to generalise from the more limited results.

Individual interview

This is a face-to-face meeting between an interviewer and a respondent. An interview may take place in a respondent's home or office, in the street, in a shopping centre, or at an arranged venue. Trained interviewers clarify difficult questions and can hold a respondent's attention for a long time.

The advantages of individual interviews are that
- they facilitate the researcher in probing the answers in depth
- the product, advertisements or packaging can be shown and the reactions and behaviour of the respondent easily observed
- in most cases, they can be conducted fairly quickly.

The disadvantages are
- high costs (they may cost much more than the cost of telephone interviews)
- the possibility of error or interviewer bias
- the reduced ability to reach a dispersed population.

Telephone survey

The respondent is interviewed by telephone, and the interview is completed during that time. The questions must be very simple and unambiguous to enable respondents to understand them quickly and without the use of visual aids. Interviewers need to be particularly skilled, as visual communication is absent. Eircom and An Post use this method.
The advantages are that
- they are easy to administer
- response rates tend to be good
- they can be conducted quickly, which reduces costs.

The disadvantages include the fact that
- it is difficult to conduct lengthy interviews
- cost per respondent is higher than with postal surveys
- increasing reluctance of general public to participate
- visual observation is not possible.

Postal survey

In postal surveys, questionnaires are sent to respondents who are encouraged to complete and return them. They are usually used when the respondents chosen for questioning are spread over a wide area and the budget for the survey is limited.

The advantages are:
- they are usually the least expensive, assuming an adequate return rate
- interviewer bias is eliminated, since the form is completed without the interviewer
- actual or promised anonymity for respondents
- they give respondents an opportunity to reply more thoughtfully, to talk to family members and so on.

The disadvantages are:
- inflexibility, as questionnaires must be short and simple for respondents to complete
- no opportunity to probe respondents to clarify or elaborate on their answers
- low response rates
- difficult to obtain a complete mailing list.

E-mail survey

As the number of Internet users grows, many businesses are now turning towards e-mail surveys. An e-mail survey is an interviewing technique in which researchers use batch-type electronic mail to send surveys to potential respondents. The respondents key in their answers and send their replies by e-mail.

The advantages of e-mail surveys are:
- e-mail is one of the applications most commonly used by Internet users
- rapid response rate
- higher response rate in comparison to postal or telephone surveys
- respondents may sometimes enquire about the meaning of particular questions or ask questions they might have.
- computer-aided interviewing (CAI) can be used.

The disadvantages include:
- every person does not have access to the Internet
- every Internet user does not necessarily use email
- people can answer an email survey more than once

- Internet users are not a randomly chosen sample of the entire population and therefore the results cannot be used to draw conclusions about large markets
- competitors could get to see online research.

Questionnaires and questionnaire design

A questionnaire is a set of questions designed to generate the data required for accomplishing the objectives of the research project. Questionnaires are the most commonly used research instrument for gathering and recording information from personal interviews, postal surveys, and telephone surveys.

The design of a questionnaire is critical to the findings of any survey. The style, length and layout of the questionnaire must be considered. The questionnaire must reflect the purpose of the research, collect the appropriate data accurately and efficiently, and facilitate the analysis of the data. An unbiased approach to composing questions is required, and questions should be clear and easy to understand. Questions should be relevant, so that the length of the questionnaire can be kept to a minimum. Only questions that will elicit data to help research the objectives of the survey should be included. Technical jargon, rarely used words and ambiguous statements must all be avoided.

Two forms of questions are used: open-ended and closed-ended. With **open-ended questions** the respondent is encouraged to answer in his or her own words. The researcher does not limit the response choices. Often open-ended questions require probing from the interviewer to encourage the respondent to elaborate or continue the discussion. The interviewer may ask, 'Is there anything else?' or 'Would you elaborate on that?' The form of such a question can be: 'What do you think about Ireland's membership of the European Union?' or 'From what you know of the proposed development, do you think the company is being open and honest about its plans or not?' Such questions allow for quality in the answer and are free of bias. The main disadvantage of open-ended questions can arise in their interpretation.

A **closed-ended question** is one that requires the respondent to make a selection from a given list of responses. The primary advantage of closed-ended questions is simply the avoidance of many of the problems of open-ended questions. Bias is removed, because the interviewer is simply ticking a box, circling a category, recording a number, or pressing a key.

Traditionally, researchers have separated the two-item response option from the many-item type. A two-choice question is called **dichotomous**; the many-item type is called **multiple choice**. An example of a dichotomous question is: 'Do you smoke?' The answer must either be yes or no. An example of a multiple-choice question is: 'Do you smoke 10–19, 20–29 or 30–39 cigarettes a day?'

Before a questionnaire is administered it should be tested on a small-scale sample so that it can be refined before the full survey goes ahead. This is known as the pilot stage, and it is very important in ensuring that the questionnaire is adequate for collecting the data required.

The advantages of questionnaires include:
- Replies tend to be more truthful because of the anonymity of respondents.
- They are useful for blanket canvassing of a wide area.
- Individual interviewer bias is eliminated.

The disadvantages include:
- Response rates are low.
- Targeted mailing lists may not be available.
- Data collection is slow.
- Questionnaires are inflexible, as further probing questions cannot be asked.

3 Experiments

Experiments are the third method researchers use in gathering data. An experiment is distinguished by the researcher's changing of one or more variables — price, packaging, design, shelf space, advertising theme, or advertising expenditures — while observing the effects of these changes on another variable (usually sales). In experiments, data is obtained by manipulating factors under tightly controlled conditions to test cause and effect. This technique is concerned with measuring the relationship between two marketing variables that are thought to be related in some way.

The objective of experiments is to measure causality. The best experiments are those in which all factors are held constant except the ones being manipulated. This enables the researcher to observe that changes in sales, for example, can be caused by changes in the amount of money spent on advertising.

Experiments may take place under laboratory conditions or in the field. McDonald's, for example, test-marketed the idea of adding a single-slice 'McPizza' to its menu. The results from the test-market cities were disappointing, and the company therefore decided to abandon the idea.

Sampling plan

The next part of the research plan to be decided on is the sampling plan. *Sampling* is the systematic choosing of a limited number of units to represent the characteristics of the total market or population. The sampling plan aims to achieve samples that are representative of the total population from which they are drawn. In this way researchers try to project the behaviour pattern of the target population without the effort and cost of surveying every consumer.

Sampling is one of the most important aspects of marketing research, because it involves the selection of respondents on which conclusions will be based. A sampling plan consists of (*a*) a sampling frame and, in the case of probability sampling, (*b*) a sample size and (*c*) a sampling method.

The **sampling frame** is a list of the population members from which the units to be sampled are selected. The researcher must first decide *who* is to be surveyed. The age, sex and other personal characteristics of potential re-spondents may be relevant, depending on the objectives of the survey. All the people who are members of a sample frame for a particular survey are known as the 'population'. For example, a telephone directory might be the sample frame for a telephone survey sample. This example shows that there is seldom a perfect correspondence between the sampling frame and the population of interest. The population of interest might be all households in a city. The telephone directory, however, would not include those households that do not have telephones, or have ex-directory numbers.

Once the sampling frame has been chosen, the researcher must then decide *how many* people are to be surveyed. The process of determining **sample size** for probability samples involves financial, statistical and managerial consider-ations. Other things being equal, the larger the sample, the smaller the sampling error. However, larger samples cost more money. Frequently the sample size for a project is determined by the budget. Financial constraints challenge the researcher to develop research designs that will generate data of adequate quality for decision-making purposes when resources are limited.

In determining the **sampling method**, the researcher must decide whether to use **probability sampling** or **non-probability sampling**. A **probability sample** is characterised by every element in the population having a known probability of being selected. Such samples allow the researcher to estimate how much sampling error is present in a given study. **Non-probability samples** include all samples that cannot be considered probability samples. Specifically, any sample in which little or no attempt is made to ensure that a representative cross-section of the population is obtained can be considered a non-probability sample. The researchers cannot statistically calculate the reliability of the sample: that is to say, they cannot determine the degree of sampling error that can be expected.

(a) Probability sampling

Random sampling is considered to be the purest form of probability sample. Random sampling provides each member of the population with an equal and known chance of being selected for the sample. As each member of the population has an equal chance of being selected, and there is no bias in the selection process, this sampling procedure enables researchers to gain a very accurate reflection of the views of the population. Random sampling is appealing because it seems simple and meets all the necessary requirements of a probability sample.

(b) Stratified sampling

Stratified samples are probability samples that are distinguished by the following procedural steps. Firstly, the original population is divided into two or more mutually exclusive and exhaustive sub-sets (for example male and female). Secondly, random samples of elements from the two or more sub-sets are chosen independently from each other.

Stratified samples are used rather than random samples because of their potential for greater statistical efficiency. This means that if there are two samples from the same population, one a properly stratified sample and the other a random sample, the stratified sample will have a smaller sampling error.

Area sampling is an alternative form of stratified sampling, where the population is divided into mutually exclusive geographical groups (such as parishes or district electoral divisions), and the researcher selects sample areas or clusters to be surveyed. However, because of the high costs and logistical difficulties of finding a random sample, non-probability sampling is far more common.

(c) Non-probability sampling

Judgmental sampling is the term given to any situation in which the researcher is attempting to draw a representative sample based on judgmental selection criteria. Judgmental samples are selected deliberately by researchers because they believe the respondents represent better sources of accurate information. Many product tests conducted in shopping centres are essentially judgmental samples. The shopping centres used for product taste tests, for example, are selected according to the researcher's judgment that they attract a reasonable cross-section of consumers who fall into the target group for the product being tested.

(d) Quota sampling

Quota samples are typically selected in such a way that demographic characteristics of interest to the researcher are represented in the sample in the same proportions as they are in the population. The researcher decides that a certain proportion of the total sample should comprise respondents conforming to selected characteristics in order to cut down bias.

Step 3: Data collection

At this stage the researcher is ready to put the research plan (step 2) into action. The collection of the data may be done by the company's marketing research staff or by outside research agencies. Interviewers must be briefed and trained for face-to-face and telephone data collection, and administrative systems must be set up for mail surveys. This stage of the process is often the most expensive and the one most subject to mistakes or problems. It is essential, therefore, that the researcher monitors closely all aspects of the fieldwork to ensure the accuracy of data collection, as important decisions may be determined by the results.

Step 4: Data analysis

This stage involves turning the 'raw data' (that is, the responses given on the questionnaires) into useful information. A researcher must remember that it is on the basis of this analysis that important decisions are likely to be made.

The researcher will first tabulate the data and then analyse them. He or she must calculate what the average is, and then measure what deviates from the average. The data must be cross-tabulated in an attempt to produce useful relationships. These types of investigation can be undertaken with relative ease, provided the data have been entered properly into appropriate computer programs. It is still, however, the researcher's own expertise, for example in identifying a trend that provides the essential component for marketing managers, that transforms the data into valuable information.

Step 5: Presentation of report and recommendations

At this final stage, conclusions have to be drawn from the findings to create information that relates to the objectives set, and this information has to be communicated to marketing decision-makers. The report is then presented orally and followed by a discussion.

The report should recount the issues and deal with the principal findings. The final outcome of the investigation is the researchers' conclusions and recommendations. The presentation of the findings should include

- the purpose of the research: for whom and by whom it was undertaken
- a general description of what was covered
- the size, nature of sample and date of execution of the fieldwork
- the research methods employed
- a description of staff and control methods
- a copy of the questionnaire
- factual data findings.

The layout of the final report should be as follows:
- title page
- table of contents
- preface
- executive summary
- research methods
- findings
- conclusions
- recommendations
- appendixes.

Important terms and concepts

information: p. 69
data: p. 69
marketing information system: p. 70
elements of the MIS: p. 70
internal records: p. 71
marketing intelligence: p. 71
information analysis: p. 71
marketing research: p. 71
quantitative information: p. 72
qualitative information: p. 72
marketing research process: p. 73
research objectives: p. 74
exploratory research: p. 74
descriptive research: p. 74
causal research: p. 74
research plan: p. 75
primary data: p. 75
secondary data: p. 75
internal data: p. 75
external data: p. 75
observation: p. 76
mechanical observation: p. 77
surveys: p. 77
focus groups: p. 77

individual interview: p. 78
telephone survey: p. 78
postal survey: p. 79
e-mail survey: p. 79
questionnaires: p. 80
open-ended questions: p. 80
closed-ended questions: p. 80
dichotomous: p. 80
multiple choice: p. 80
experiments: p. 81
sampling plan: p. 81
sampling: p. 81
sampling frame: p. 82
sampling methods: p. 82
probability sampling: p. 82
non-probability sampling: p. 82
random sampling: p. 82
stratified sampling: p. 83
judgmental sampling: p. 83
quota sampling: p. 83
data collection: p. 84
data analysis: p. 84
presenting the report: p. 84

Case Study: Marketing research and Cadbury

Marketing research is a process designed to link managers with consumers through information. It is used to identify opportunities and make better-informed decisions about products that have future market potential. Marketing research has revealed that snacks play more of a functional role than one of pure indulgence: they are often a meal substitute. It has also been shown that successful snack brands in the confectionary category tend to have more 'foody' values and often contain ingredients such as wafer, cereal, peanuts, biscuits and fruit to break up the chocolate delivery.

Cadbury's philosophy is to continue as a driving force in the confectionary market, and therefore constantly analyse its offerings to consumers. The 'Fuse' concept was developed after marketing research identified the growth of snacking and a definite gap in the market for a more chocolatey snack. A number of ingredients were devised and tested following a survey, which asked consumers about their snacking habits and preferences. A Research and Development team then developed some product recipes, which addressed the needs of the respondents.

A lot of development time was spent on Fuse. More than 250 ingredients were tried and tested in various combinations before the recipe was finalised. As a new product in the snacking market, Fuse had to establish its USP (unique selling proposition), which would not be shared by any of its competitors. Therefore, the product developers decided to use Cadbury's chocolate to 'fuse' together a number of popular snacking ingredients such as peanuts, raisins, crisp cereal and fudge pieces.

Fuse went through two extensive 'in home placement' tests. The results of these tests enabled Cadbury to anticipate the volume of bars required for the launch of Fuse and post-launch. Research is vital throughout the product-development process. In the pre-launch research tests, Fuse scored higher for texture, 'interesting to eat' and combination of ingredients, than its competitors and achieved the highest rating ever for a new Cadbury product – 82% of consumers rated Fuse as excellent or very good and 83% said they would buy it regularly. Within the first three months of its launch 70 million Fuse bars were purchased.

Source: http://www.cadbury.co.uk

Case Study: Solving marketing problems through research: Lansdowne

Lansdowne Market Research, established in 1979, is the largest ad hoc marketing research agency in Ireland. It is a fully independent Irish company with a permanent staff of 55. The company carries out research for most of Ireland's major companies and multinationals. It has extensive experience of a wide variety of markets, especially the service industry, media, FMCG (Fast Moving Consumer Goods) and retail. It also has a strong international focus, with one in four of its projects being undertaken for foreign-based companies. In 2005, it undertook over 450 projects on behalf of 170 different clients.

Lansdowne's company philosophy is 'to provide added-value research and a pragmatic approach to solving marketing problems and aiding strategy development.' It believes in a combination of high quality but cost-effective surveys, with creative and added-value analysis. Its management is based on a team structure within a corporate culture so as to stimulate close interrelationship and exchange of ideas for the benefit of its clients. In order to have a flexible environment, it encourages its researchers to be dualists, with both qualitative and quantitative expertise.

So what type of research projects does Lansdowne undertake?

- Customer Satisfaction surveys based on face-to-face and computer aided telephone interviews (CATI) in the financial, automotive, telecommunications, information technology and tourism sectors.
- Media: since 1989, Lansdowne has been the contractor for the National Readership Survey in Ireland – the JNRR (Joint National Readership Research, the largest random probability survey carried out in the Republic of Ireland. It is used as a basis for buying and selling advertising space in Irish newspapers and magazines.
- Other media research includes: ongoing monitoring of cinema attendance; evaluation for potential for new radio stations; ongoing attitude surveys to TV programme content and presenters; image surveys for a Sunday newspaper.
- Omnibus: a cost-effective way of tracking consumer purchasing, awareness and attitude trends. Lansdowne runs the largest Omnibus in the Republic of Ireland. It conducts personal in-home interviews with over 30,000 adults aged 15+ and covers over 150 different topics each year, on a fortnightly basis.
- Telebus: a monthly service launched in May 2001. This telephone interviewing service is a network extension of the Omnibus survey.
- Polling: it successfully pioneered the first Exit Poll for a General Election in Ireland in 1997. This involved carrying out an exit survey among 3,000

voters in a wide variety of polling stations, immediately after they had voted. The predictions of the outcome were then delivered to RTE. It also carries out polls for presidential and European Parliament elections, etc.

- Socio-political research: Lansdowne has been the contractor for over 12 years for the European Union's face-to-face Eurobarometer survey in Ireland.
- Qualitative research: focus groups and in-depth interviews account for one in four of all the projects it undertakes.
- AD & Brand Tracking: advertising and brand image tracking surveys, mainly for multinational companies, for example Adwatch April 2005.
- Product testing: New Product testing, New Format Testing, New Pack Design Testing, etc.

Source: www.lansdownemarketresearch.ie

Questions for review

1. Distinguish between marketing information systems, marketing research, and marketing intelligence.
2. Describe the typical steps in designing and conducting a marketing research assignment. Use a company of your choice to outline how each step might be conducted.
3. Discuss the various methods of collecting primary data that a company might use.
4. Outline the various sampling methods.
5. Compare and contrast primary and secondary data.
6. Distinguish between qualitative and quantitative information.
7. List some sources of secondary data.
8. What is the difference between open-ended and closed-ended questions?
9. What are the advantages and disadvantages of telephone surveys?

6
SEGMENTATION, TARGETING AND POSITIONING

Chapter objectives

After reading this chapter you should be able to
- discuss the purpose of segmentation
- define market segmentation, targeting, and positioning
- describe the main methods of segmenting markets
- identify market coverage strategies.

6.1 *The purpose of segmentation*

'Market segmentation is the process of grouping customers in markets with some heterogeneity into smaller, more similar or homogeneous segments' (Dibb et al., 1997). The basic principle of segmentation is the division of the market into distinct groups of buyers who might require separate products or marketing mixes. Market segmentation therefore consists of dividing the total market into a number of smaller sub-markets or segments. Market segmentation and diversity are complementary concepts. Without a diverse marketplace composed of many different people with different backgrounds, countries of origin, interests, needs and wants, and perceptions, there would be little reason to segment markets. Diversity in the global marketplace makes market segmentation an attractive, viable, and potentially highly profitable strategy.

In the mass-marketing era of the 1950s, multinational companies such as Coca-Cola had the power to sell large quantities of standardised goods to a 'homogeneous' mass market. Markets have changed considerably since then. Coca-Cola now offers caffeine-free, diet, cherry and other variations that combine some or all of these attributes. The increase in the variety of products offered can be seen as an attempt to meet customers' needs more precisely.

Market segmentation has also been adopted by retailers. An example is Gap, Inc. Gap (www.gap.com) targets different age, income, and lifestyle segments in a diversity of retail outlets. Gap targets upscale consumers through its Banana Republic stores and somewhat downscale consumers with its Old Navy Clothing Company stores. It targets young parents (who are also likely to be Gap of Banana Republic shoppers) with its Baby Gap and Gap Kids stores.

According to Zikmund and d'Amico (1996), the assumptions underlying segmentation are:

- Not all buyers are alike.
- Sub-groups of people with similar backgrounds, behaviour, values and needs can be identified.
- The sub-groups will be smaller and more homogeneous than the market as a whole.
- It should be easier to satisfy smaller groups of similar customers than large groups of dissimilar customers.

Marketers are usually able to cluster similar customers into specific market segments with different, and sometimes unique, demands. The number of market segments in the total market depends on the ingenuity and creativity employed in identifying those segments. In the toothpaste market, for example, companies have identified a number of segments and have targeted various groups, such as children and smokers. In general, the purpose of segmenting the market is to enable the company to concentrate its efforts on pleasing one group of people with similar needs, rather than trying to please everybody using a standard product and therefore perhaps ending up pleasing very few.

There are three stages in market segmentation, as illustrated in fig. 6.1.

Stage 1: Segmentation

- choose bases or variables for market segmentation
- profile the emerging segments
- validate the emerging segments

⇩

Stage 2: Targeting

- choose a targeting strategy
- determine how many segments are to be targeted

⇩

Stage 3: Positioning

- position products or services in the mind of consumers
- satisfy consumers' perceptions

Fig. 6.1: *Three stages in market segmentation*

6.2 *Bases or variables for segmenting the consumer market*

There is rarely a single or best way to segment a market. There are many bases or variables for segmenting the consumer market, but the following are the main ones:

- geographical
- psychographic
- behavioural
- demographic.

Geographical segmentation means dividing the market into different geographical units, such as countries, regions, counties, cities, urban, or rural. Geographical segmentation may be carried out for a number of reasons: for example, the product may be suited to people living in a specific area because of the climate. In Mediterranean countries the demand for sun protection products is greater than in Scandinavian countries.

When Campbell's launched its canned nacho sauce in the US market, it found that it was too hot for Americans in the East and not hot enough for those in the West and Southwest. As a result, its plants in Texas and California now produce a hotter nacho sauce to serve their regions than that produced in the other plants. Some marketing scholars have argued that direct-mail catalogues, free-phone numbers, satellite television transmission, global communication networks, and especially the Internet have erased all regional boundaries and that geographic segmentation should be replaced by a single global marketing strategy. Clearly, any company that decides to put its catalogue on the Internet makes is easy for individuals all over the world to browse and become customers. For consumers who shop on the Internet, it often makes little difference if online retailers are around the corner or halfway around the world – the only factor that differs is the shipping charge.

Psychographic segmentation means dividing the consumer market according to social class, life-style, or personality. Holiday companies often use life-style to segment the market, for example cruises versus inter-railing.

Social class reflects the ways people think and the beliefs they hold. It affects the ways in which people spend their money and the value they place on different types of products, for example, clothing, food, furniture, etc. Lifestyle has been defined by Kotler (1988) as: 'the person's pattern of living in the world as expressed in [their] activities, interests and opinions…[it] portrays the "whole person" interacting with his or her environment'. For example, one of the Russian ethnic groups, the Cossacks, are seen as ambitious, high spending, extroverted and preoccupied by brand names. They like driving BMWs, smoking Dunhill cigarettes and drinking Scotch. Personality reflects a person's traits, attitudes and habits. In the US in the late 1950s, both Ford and Chevrolet emphasised the brand personalities of their products in order to appeal to distinct consumer personalities. Buyers of Fords, for example, were identified as 'independent, masculine and impulsive' while Chevrolet owners were seen as 'conservative, thrifty and less masculine'. The psychographic profile of a consumer can be thought of as a combination of consumers' measured activities, interests, and opinions (**AIOs**). As an approach to constructing consumer psychographic profiles, AIO research seeks consumers' responses to a large number of statements that measure activities (how the consumer of family spends time, e.g. playing games, watching television, gardening), interests (the consumer's or family's preferences and priorities, e.g. foreign travel, fashion, food), and opinions (how the consumer feels about a wide variety of events and political issues, such as social, economic, and environmental issues). It is quite possible that people with similar demographic and/or psychographic profiles may interact differently with the same product. Segmenting a market in these terms, therefore, is known as **behavioural segmentation**.

Behavioural segmentation means dividing the market according to consumers' behaviour, knowledge, and benefits required from a product. Clothes companies, such as Gucci and Gap, use behavioural segmentation to divide the market.

Behavioural segmentation also includes usage rate (e.g. light user, medium user, heavy user), user status (e.g. non-user, ex-user, potential user, first-time user, regular user), readiness to buy (e.g. unaware, aware, informed, interested, desirous, intending to buy), brand familiarity (e.g. recognition, non-recognition, rejection), or time of buying (e.g. Christmas, Easter, Valentine's Day, birthdays, etc.). As with usage rate, loyalty could be a useful mechanism, not only for developing detail in the segment profile, but also for developing a better understanding of which segmentation variables are significant. Companies can profile consumers who are 'loyal to us', 'loyal to competitors' and **'switchers'**, and then discover what other factors seem to differentiate between each of these groups.

Demographic segmentation means dividing the market into groups according to age, gender, occupation, religion, nationality, and family size. The grocery sector has designed individual and multi-pack products, such as yoghurts and toilet rolls. Demographic segmentation is the most commonly used method of segmenting markets, because it is easy to get the relevant information about the segmenting variables.

Typically, demographic segmentation includes age breakdown such as: 18-24, 25-34, 35-49, 50-64, 65 and over. Family size breakdown normally includes: young single; young married, no children; full nest; empty nest. Companies such as Fisher Price give full recognition to the differences that exist between children of various ages, with the result that toys are now being designed to fall into specific age categories. This makes the task of choosing toys much easier for parents, relatives and friends. On the negative side, demographics are purely descriptive and, used alone, assume that all people in the same demographic group have similar needs and wants. In most cases, however, the main use of demographic segmentation is as a foundation for other more customer-focused segmentation methods.

Mass-market strategy/total market approach/ undifferentiated strategy

A company that uses this type of market coverage strategy deliberately ignores any differences that exist within its markets and decides instead to focus upon a feature that appears to be common or acceptable to a wide variety of customers. One marketing mix is used for the entire market. A company that adopts this strategy assumes that individual customers have similar needs that can be met with a common marketing mix. At one time, Coca-Cola used this strategy with a single product and a single size of its familiar green bottle. Marketers of commodity products, such as sugar and flour, are also likely to use the mass-market strategy.

Advantages:

- potential savings on production costs as only one product is produced
- marketing costs may be lower when there is only one product to promote and a single channel of distribution.

Disadvantages:

- it makes the company more susceptible to competition
- unimaginative products may be produced.

Single segment/niche/concentrated strategy

This is when a company selects one segment of a market for targeting its marketing efforts. As it is appealing to one segment, it can concentrate on understanding the needs of that particular segment and on developing and maintaining a highly specialised marketing mix. Small companies often use this strategy to compete effectively with much larger firms. The key to this strategy is 'specialisation'.

Advantages:

- strong positioning
- allows small companies to compete with larger companies better
- can meet the needs of a narrowly defined segment better
- concentration of resources
- can control costs by advertising and distributing only to the segment it views as its primary target.

Disadvantages:

- the company can be vulnerable if powerful competitors turn their attention to that niche
- segment may become too small or change due to forces in the marketing environment.

Multi-segment/multiple niche strategy/differentiated approach

This is when the firm focuses upon a variety of different segments and then develops a different marketing mix for each. It is often referred to as the 'rifle' rather than the 'shotgun' approach in that the firm can focus on buyers it has the greatest chance of satisfying rather than scattering the marketing effort. For example, the Burton Group developed and refined a highly segmented strategy during the 1980s. It paid particular attention to a variety of distinct customer groups by means of different types of retail outlets, each with its own distinct target market, image and customer appeal, i.e. Top Shop, Top Man, Principles for Women, Principles for Men, Principles for Children, etc.

Advantages:

- greater scope for expansion and growth than concentrated strategy
- greater financial success
- economies of scale in production and marketing.

Disadvantages:

- requires a high level of marketing expertise
- higher marketing costs than concentrated strategy
- cannibalisation.

6.3 *Bases or variables for segmenting the industrial market*

Industrial or organisational markets may be segmented by using variables similar to those used for segmenting the consumer market. The aim of industrial segmentation is to satisfy the needs of companies for products. The following are the most common bases used for segmenting the industrial market.

Geographical location is useful for reaching industries that are concentrated in certain places, and it enables salespeople to make the best use of their travelling time.

Operational characteristics, such as company size, industry type, and technology, also play an important role in segmenting the corporate market. IBM, for example, segments its market according to the industry in which its customers operate, with some salespeople specialising in serving the requirements of bankers, insurers, and other industries.

Purchase behaviour and usage rate are also used to segment the industrial market. Purchasing companies that use large quantities of products will expect a different service from that received by customers who buy only small quantities.

6.4 *Requirements for a usable segment*

There is no limit to the numbers of ways in which a market can be segmented; but if a segment is to be successfully exploited it must fulfil the following requirements:

- It must be *measurable* or *definable*. This means there must be some way of identifying the members of the segment and knowing how many are in the segment.
- It must be *substantial*. This means it must be large enough to be sufficiently profitable to justify developing and maintaining a specific marketing mix.
- It must be *accessible*. This means the segment must be easy to reach with the developed marketing mix, and communication with the segment as a group must be achievable.

- It must be *stable*. This means the nature of the segment must be reasonably constant, so that marketers can make strategic decisions knowing that the segment, as such, will survive long enough.

6.5 *The advantages of market segmentation*

Segmenting the market allows companies to have a better understanding of customers' needs, wants, and demands, and allows them to keep in touch and to respond quickly to changes demanded by their chosen segment.

It also allows the marketer to spot market opportunities, for example if a segment is unhappy with the existing products or services.

Market segmentation also allows for more effective use of a company's resources, for example improved budget allocation for specific market segments. The obvious gain to consumers is that they can find products that seem to fit more closely with what they want. Consumers may feel that a particular company is more sympathetic towards them, or is speaking more directly to them, and therefore they will be more responsive and eventually more loyal to that company.

Market segmentation helps the organisation to target its marketing mix more closely on the potential consumer, and thus to meet the consumer's needs and wants more exactly. Segmentation helps to define shopping habits (in terms of place, frequency and volume), price sensitivity, required product benefits and features, as well as laying the foundation for advertising and promotional decisions.

Segmentation can also help the company to allocate its resources more efficiently. If a segment is well defined, then the company will have sufficient understanding to develop very precise marketing objectives and an accompanying strategy to achieve them, with a minimum of wastage.

Finally, the use of segmentation will help the organisation to achieve a better understanding of itself and the environment within which it exists. By looking outwards, to the consumer, the company has to ask itself some very difficult questions about its capacity to serve that consumer better than the competition.

Dangers of segmentation
Catering for differing needs of a large number of segments can lead to fragmentation of the market, with additional problems arising from the loss of economies of scale (e.g. through shorter production runs or loss of bulk purchasing discounts on raw materials).

Within the market as a whole, if there are a number of companies in direct competition for a number of segments, then the potential proliferation of brands may simply serve to confuse the consumer.

6.6 *Targeting*

Having divided the market into segments, companies must decide which segment will be the best to target, given the overall objectives of the company. Normally, a company would choose the most profitable segment, but equally a company may decide to aim for a particular segment of the market which is currently neglected, on the grounds that competitors are less likely to enter the market. The process of selecting a segment to aim for is called *targeting*. Choosing the right market and then targeting it accurately are two of the most important activities a marketer carries out. Choosing the wrong segment to target, or not attempting to segment the market at all leads to lost opportunities and wasted effort. Targeting is the deliberate selection of segments by a company for its sales and marketing efforts. After carrying out detailed market research, it can then decide what to offer the target market. A marketer has to consider the following:

- What do the consumers in the target segment need and want?
- What is already available to them?
- What can the company offer that would be better than what is now available?
- What is the intensity of the competition?
- What company resources are available?
- What is the size of the company's existing market share?

    According to Abell (1980), there are three basic market coverage strategies, as shown in Table 6.1.

	Definition	Example
Mass-market strategy	A company enters every possible segment of its potential market.	Pepsi-Cola Kelloggs
Single segment or niche strategy	A company directs its marketing effort towards a single market segment.	Mercedes-Benz Rolls-Royce
Multi-segment strategy	A company directs its marketing efforts towards two or more market segments.	British Airways

Table 6.1: *Market coverage strategies*

6.7 *Positioning*

Positioning has been defined by Wind (1984) as 'the place a product occupies in a given market, as perceived by the relevant group of customers; that group of customers is known as the target segment of the market.'

A product's position is the place the product occupies in the minds of the consumers. Positioning, therefore, is the process of creating an image for a product in the minds of target customers. Consumers build up a position for a product based on what they expect and believe to be the most likely features of the product. Marketers therefore need to find out what the most important features of the product are in the minds of the consumer. They can adjust their marketing mix to give the product its most effective position relative to competitors. Many marketers try to convey the clear advantages of their products over competing brands, as for example with Dunnes Stores' slogan, 'The difference is—we're Irish.'

According to Ries and Trout (1981), 'positioning is not what you do to a product; positioning is what you do to the mind of the prospect.' This emphasises the fact that the most important issue is the perception and evaluation by the potential customers of all those things that are done in marketing a product or service. Potential customers need to know

- that the product or service exists
- where it can be bought
- that they can afford it
- that it is likely to meet the needs for which it is required.

This means that when positioning their products, marketers must ensure that the 'four As' are met:

- awareness
- availability
- affordability
- acceptability.

Awareness is influenced by advertising, promotions, branding, display, and personal selling. *Availability* depends on distribution and physical handling. *Affordability* depends on pricing. *Acceptability* is influenced by packaging and quality. One obvious way of making a product or service more acceptable is by adding extra features to the core product.

Positioning is an important element of the marketing planning process, since any decision on positioning has direct and immediate implications for the entire marketing mix. The marketing mix can be seen, therefore, as the tactical details of the firm's positioning strategy. For example, if a firm is pursuing a high-quality position, this needs to be reflected in the quality of the product and also in every element of the marketing mix, including price, distribution, the type of promotion and the after-sales service. Without this consistency, the credibility of the positioning strategy is dramatically reduced. Porsche, for example, is positioned in the prestige segment of the car market with a differential advantage based on performance.

Steps for Positioning:

1. Identify the attributes/characteristics used by consumers in a segment to understand brands.
2. Locate the firm's brand relative to other brands, based on how it is perceived by buyers.
3. Identify the ideal position for consumers in that segment.
4. Decide the best way to position the firm's product.
5. Develop the marketing mix that supports the positioning strategy the firm has selected.

In summary, positioning is developing a distinct image for the product or service in the mind of the consumer, an image that will differentiate the offering from competing ones and communicate to consumers that the particular product or service will fulfil their needs better than competing brands. Positioning is more important to the ultimate success of a product than are its actual characteristics, although products that are poorly made will not succeed in the long run on the basis of image alone. The core of effective positioning is a unique position that the product occupies in the mind of the consumer. Most new products fail because they are perceived as 'me too' offerings that do not offer potential consumers any advantages or unique benefits over competitive products.

The result of a successful positioning strategy is a distinctive brand image on which consumers rely in making product choices. A positive brand image also leads to consumer loyalty, positive beliefs about brand value, and a willingness to search for the brand. A positive brand image also promotes consumer interest in future brand promotions.

Important terms and concepts

Case Study: Market segmentation: Nivea Sun

Nivea is one of the family of brands owned by Beirsdorf, the international skincare company. Nivea targets different market segments to meet individual consumer needs. Nivea products range from female products to men's shaving gels, deodorants and sun care lines. The three main ways in which the sun care market is segmented reflect the reasons why people buy products:

- Protection – Nivea Sun provides products that enable people to protect themselves from the harmful effects of the sun. It is the market leader by value in this segment. This segment can be further divided according to skin type and location (both factors will affect the level of protection needed, for example, the effects of the sun are harsher in the tropics).
- After Sun – this is a rapidly expanding market segment.
- Self-tan – tanning products used for cosmetic appeal.

Nivea Sun's brand vision is 'To be the number 1 brand in the UK sun market in penetration, sales and likeability'. Penetration means how many potential consumers in a segment actually purchase or uses the product. Sales are measured by value or volume and likeability refers to whether the brand is enjoyed. Nivea Sun strives for the vision by continually segmenting consumer markets.

Nivea Sun's main methods of segmentation are by *demographics,* referring to the different characteristics of populations, and *attitudes,* referring to why people buy products. Nivea Sun's market research has identified different types of users. People were asked when they used a sun care product (e.g. holiday, sports) and why. The first relates to the Sun Protection Factor (SPF) required, the second to the type (e.g. a spray or a product for children. There are five main types of buyer:

- Concerned consumers have protection as a priority.
- Sun avoiders, who prefer to stay out of the sun rather than protect against it. This segment need easy-to-use products.
- Sun lovers are consumers who adore sunshine and know about protection. These consumers need a brand they can trust and are loyal to that brand.
- Careless tanners – like the sun but do not protect properly.
- Beauty conscious – want a good sun tan, know protection is important, but do not really understand SPFs.

Nivea Sun's brand strategy is based on the key proposition of protection. It also concentrates on making sun care simpler and educating about the dangers of the sun. Product launches have therefore included spray products that are easy to apply (aimed at men), coloured products to be more fun (aimed at children) and products offering better protection. The education message is reinforced through advertising and a school educational programme. A 'Sun Sense' primary school pack goes out to 10,000 teachers each year.

In summary, by knowing about its market segments, Nivea Sun can target them successfully. Segmentation enables Nivea Sun to stay as the number 1 protection and after sun brand in terms of value sales in the UK.

Source: http://www.thetimes100.co.uk/studies

Case Study: Florette 'raw passion' in a bag – catering for busy lifestyles

Irish consumers have an ever increasing appetite for tasty, healthy and convenient food. Florette, the salad market leader promises to deliver 'raw passion' in a bag to health conscious consumers. The concept of washed and ready to eat salads in a bag was virtually unknown in Europe up to recent years. Today, the Florette brand – part of a co-operative of farmers and growers in the Cotentin region of northwest France – is widely recognised. Florette arrived in Ireland in June 2000, and it has mirrored its success in prepared salads in the UK and it now has 37% by value of the Irish market.

Five years ago bagged salads used to be an impulse product but that has changed, and that trend is one that business manager for Florette in Ireland, Thomas Dewez is keen to build on. 'Irish tastes have become more discerning and people are choosing less traditional salads in an attempt to recreate a "dining out" experience at home. I think the smoking ban has had an impact.

People used to go out, have lunch, have a drink, and could smoke in a pub or a restaurant. I am not saying that everybody is eating at home but there is a trend there. People like to prepare a meal accompanied by a nice salad, a nice wine, and invite friends over. It fits in with a more European lifestyle'.

Health and convenience are two of Florette's key attributes. Florette believe that with current healthy eating trends the bagged salad market will continue to have strong sales growth. The products are packed in five factories across Europe, including a facility in Lichfield in England. Florette's factory in Lichfield currently supplies the Irish market, and operates to high standards to ensure the product reaches the consumer as fresh as possible. An innovative cutting robot is used to reduce handling, and leaves are inspected with care manually. Leaves are washed twice in pure water after cleaning.

Dewez points out that while salad is a seasonal product, it is becoming popular all year round. The summer, however, remains a very busy time and demand goes up because of barbecues and good weather. 'The start of season for us would be when the weather gets a bit milder; the end of season is towards the end of September when kids are back to school. But, during Christmas week, we sell more product than summer'. Florette's best selling product in Ireland is its crispy salad, second is mixed salad. According to Dewez 'Salad dressing is also part of our development as dressing is now something we see regularly on the shopping list which previously might have been considered an impulse purchase on buying bagged salad. To cater for the busy lifestyle we introduced a small bag of salad with one serving so that there is no waste'.

Source: www.checkout.ie

Questions for review

1. Identify and describe the variables or bases that can be used to segment *consumer* markets. Give examples of products that are segmented by such variables.
2. Describe the conditions required for effective segmentation.
3. What are the main methods used to segment industrial or corporate markets?
4. Define (*a*) segmentation, (*b*) targeting, and (*c*) positioning, and give examples of companies that practise each of these activities.
5. Distinguish between the three basic market coverage strategies. Illustrate your answer with appropriate examples.
6. What are the advantages of market segmentation?
7. Why do companies segment markets?

8. List the difference between single segment and multi-segment strategies.
9. Choose a product and describe how it could be best positioned in the market.

7
PRODUCT

Chapter objectives

After reading this chapter you should be able to
* understand product classification
* recognise the importance of brands
* outline the benefits of packaging and labelling
* describe the stages of the product life-cycle
* describe the new-product development process.

7.1 *The product*

The product is at the heart of the marketing exchange. If the product does not deliver the benefits the customer wanted or if it does not live up to the expectations created by the other elements of the marketing mix, then the whole exercise has been in vain. Consumers buy products to solve problems or to enhance their lives and thus the marketer has to ensure that the product can fully satisfy the consumer, not just in functional terms, but also in psychological terms. The product is important, therefore, because it is the ultimate test of whether the organisation has understood its customer's needs. A *product* is a good, service, or idea. It consists of a bundle of tangible and intangible attributes, including physical, social and psychological utilities, that satisfies consumers, and is received in an exchange. Murray and O'Driscoll (1998) define a product as 'a bundle of physical, service and psychological benefits designed to satisfy a customer's needs and related wants.'

The *physical benefits* of a product are the tangible elements, for example a computer, including its monitor, keyboard, and mouse. The *service* aspect of a product represents all the product benefits that make the product saleable, for example the facilities provided, guarantees, installation, training, after-sales service, and free phone support. The *psychological benefits* of a product are its symbolic aspects, including its brand name and the company's reputation and image, creating associations with certain people and life-styles.

7.2 *Product classification*

It is useful for companies to define groups of products that have similar characteristics or that generate similar buyer behaviour within a market. Companies classify products to help develop similar marketing strategies for a wide range of products offered. There are two ways to classify products: by degree of tangibility or durability, and by type of user.

Degree of tangibility or durability

There are three main types in this category. *Durable goods* usually last for many uses and for a long time before having to be replaced, for example cars, domestic electrical goods, stereo equipment, furniture. *Non-durable goods* are consumed in one or a few uses before they have to be replaced, for example food and drink, soap, fuel, stationery. *Services* are intangible products that consist of activities, benefits or satisfactions offered for sale, for example marketing research, education, holidays, financial services, home repairs, catering.

They involve a deed, performance, or an effort that cannot be physically possessed. Services have four unique characteristics/features that distinguish them from physical goods. These four elements are referred to as the **four 'I's of services**.

1. Intangibility

The basic difference between physical goods and services is that services are intangible. They cannot be held, touched, seen, tasted or felt in the same manner in which goods can be sensed. Services cannot be stored and are often easy to duplicate. They cannot be protected through patents and prices are difficult to set. This characteristic makes it more difficult for marketers to communicate the benefits of an intangible service than to communicate the benefits of tangible goods.

2. Inseparability

The production and consumption of services are inseparable activities. This means that in most cases consumers cannot and do not separate the service from the provider of the service or the setting in which the service occurs. For example, to receive an education, a person may attend a third-level institution. The quality of the education may be high, but if the student has difficulty parking or sees little or no opportunity to take part in extracurricular activity, he/she may not be satisfied with the educational experience.

3. Inconsistency

This is also referred to as heterogeneity. It means that services tend to be less standardised and uniform than physical products. As services depend upon people to provide them, their quality varies because people have different capabilities and also vary in job performance from day to day.

4. Inventory

This is more commonly known as perishability. It means that services cannot be stored, warehoused or inventoried. An empty theatre seat or hotel room provides no revenue that day, therefore, the revenue is lost forever. On the other hand, service providers may have to turn away customers during peak periods. It is a major challenge for marketers to find ways to synchronise supply and demand.

Type of user

Consumer goods

Consumer goods are products bought by the final consumer for personal consumption.

There are four types of consumer goods, according to consumer buying habits. **Convenience goods** are consumer goods that the consumer buys frequently, conveniently, and with a minimum of buying effort, for example newspapers, toothpaste, soap, bread, chocolate. **Shopping goods** are consumer goods for which the consumer tends to shop around in order to compare quality, price, or style, for example cameras, televisions, electrical appliances, clothes, computers. **Speciality goods** are consumer goods that the customer makes a special effort to search for, for example collectors' items, works of art, jewellery, designer clothes, prestige cars. **Unsought goods** are consumer goods that the consumer either does not know about or knows about but does not at first want. These require a lot of promotional activities to stimulate sales, for example insurance, smoke-detectors, alarm systems.

Industrial goods

Industrial goods are items bought by individuals and companies for further production or support. The sale of industrial goods often results or is derived from the sale of consumer goods. **Capital items** consist of buildings, fixed equipment, portable factory equipment and office equipment that has to be installed for production to occur. **Supplies and services** are industrial goods that facilitate the production and efficient running of a company without any direct input; these include operating supplies (computer paper, paint), maintenance and repair (cleaning materials), and business services (legal advice, management consultancy, accountancy). ***Materials and parts*** are items that make up the product, either through further processing or as components; they include raw materials (crude oil, iron ore, cotton, timber, fish, fruit and vegetables) and manufactured materials and parts (cement, tyres, car batteries, yarn).

7.3 *Branding*

Branding is an important element of the tangible product and, particularly in consumer markets, as it is a means of linking items with a product line or emphasising the individuality of product items. Branding can also help in the development of a new product by facilitating the extension of a product line or mix, through building on the consumer's perceptions of the values and character represented by the brand name. This points to the most important function of branding: the creation and communication of a three-dimensional character for a product that is not easily copied or damaged by competitors' efforts. An important result of the way customers perceive a product is the recognition of a brand. A ***brand*** is a name, symbol or design that has a distinct image and that differentiates one product from another. A ***brand name*** is the verbal part of the brand, for example Ballygowan, Kerrygold, Actimel, Club Med, Disneyland. A brand or brand name can be almost anything a marketer wants it to be, but by itself it has no legal status. A ***trademark***, on the other hand, is a legally protected brand name, logo (the name of the company written in a particular way), or symbol.

The owners of trademarks have exclusive rights to their use. A strong brand, for example Guinness, is likely to prove very difficult for competitors to copy and can offer a competitive advantage over other products.

The object of branding is to attract a group of customers who are 'brand-loyal', which means that they buy the brand regularly and do not change to competing brands. Branding offers advantages to both the consumer and the manufacturer. For the consumer it helps in identifying products and in evaluating their quality. Manufacturers also benefit from branding, because each company's brand identifies its products, and this makes repeat buying easier for consumers. Branding helps a company to introduce a new product that carries the name of one or more of its existing products, because consumers are already familiar with the company's existing brands. '*It is my conviction that what we call shareholder value is best defined by how strongly employees and customers feel about your brand. Nothing seems more obvious to me than that a product or service only becomes a brand when it is imbued with profound values that translate into fact and feelings that employees can project and customers embrace'* (Richard Branson of Virgin Airlines, 2000).

According to Ries (1995), brand names should have the following characteristics:

- They should attract the customer's attention.
- They should be memorable.
- They should be linked to a visual image.
- They should communicate something about the product, or be capable of being used to communicate something about the product.
- They should be 'telephone-friendly'.

7.4 *Types of brands*

Family branding involves using a single brand name, such as Campbell's, Del Monte, or Heinz, over a whole line of fairly closely related items. The idea of family branding is to take advantage of a brand's reputation and the good will associated with the name. The use of family branding, however, does not guarantee success in the market. A company's other products may suffer because of problems with a product sold under the same brand name. This is one reason why some companies use individual brand names rather than family brand names.

An *individual brand* is assigned to a product within a product line that is not shared by other products in that line. Some companies use the individual branding approach because they wish to market several products that appeal to different market segments. Companies such as Procter and Gamble, for example, use individual brands for their Bold, Daz, Tide and Dreft detergents. Other companies use individual branding to capture shelf space: for example, the Mars company produces Snickers, Milky Way, M&Ms, and many others; therefore, if a retailer has only got space to display twenty brands and ten of them are Mars brands, the chances that a customer will select a Mars product are much improved.

Own-label brands are developed by wholesalers or retailers. The main characteristic of own-label brands is that the manufacturers are not identified on the product. Own-label brands give wholesalers or retailers the freedom to buy products at the lowest cost without disclosing the identity of the manufacturer. Familiar retailer brand names include *St Bernard* (Dunnes Stores), *St Michael* (Marks & Spencer), and *Primark* (Penneys).

A **generic brand** indicates only the product category, for example aluminium foil, and does not include the name of the company, manufacturer, or distributor. The goods are plainly packaged with stark lettering that simply lists the contents. Usually generic brands are sold at prices below those of comparable branded items.

According to Dibb et al. (1997), successful brands must

- give priority to quality
- offer superior service
- get there first
- differentiate brands
- develop a unique positioning concept
- have a strong communication programme
- be consistent and reliable.

It is important for marketers to know if a particular brand is successful in order to capture the leading share in its market segment. If a brand is not successful, marketers need to consider removing it from their company's product range.

7.5 *The benefits of branding*

Branding is of particular value to the buyer in a complex and crowded marketplace. In a supermarket, for example, brand names and visual images make it easier to locate and identify required products. Strong branding can help consumers judge whether it is their sort of product, delivering the functional and psychological benefits sought. This is particularly true for a new, untried product. Strong brands also strengthen the relationship between the consumer and the manufacturing company.

The manufacturer's key interest in branding is in the building of brand loyalty to the point where the trust, liking and preference for the brand overcome any doubts regarding price sensitivity, thus allowing a reasonable measure of premium pricing and the prevention of brand switching.

Other benefits of branding for the manufacturer are linked with segmentation and competitive positioning strategies. Different brands can be used by one organisation to target different segments. Because the different brands have clearly defined individual characteristics, the consumer does not necessarily link them and thus does not become confused about what the organisation stands for.

Strong branding is also important for providing competitive advantage, not just in terms of generating consumer loyalty, but also as a means of competing head-on, competing generally across the whole market in an almost undifferentiated way or finding a niche in which to dominate.

7.6 *Packaging and labelling*

Packaging

The *packaging* element of a product refers to any container or wrapping in which it is offered for sale and on which information is communicated. It is an expensive and important part of a company's marketing strategy. Packaging not only serves a functional purpose, but also acts as a means of communicating product information and brand character. The packaging is often the consumer's first point of contact with the actual product so it is essential to make it attractive and appropriate for both the product's and the consumer's needs.

The benefits of packaging

Functional benefits: Packaging plays an important functional role. It protects the product in storage, in shipment, and on display (by extending its shelf life) and prevents tampering. It also helps to increase convenience for the consumer, as for example with toothpaste sold in pump dispensers, ring-pulls on soft drink cans, resealable packets of sliced meat (Denny's cooked ham).

Communication benefits: Packaging conveys information to the consumer on the composition and optimum use of the product, for example, cooking instructions may accompany ingredients.

Perceptual benefits: Packaging creates a perception in the consumer's mind. It can imply status, economy, or product quality. Companies have to be careful when selecting colours for their packaging, as colour can affect consumers' perceptions. For example, in trying to modernise its image, Coca-Cola has redesigned its logo and package design but has held on to its established red-and-white colours.

Labelling

Labelling is closely related to packaging and can be used to display legally required information, for example regulations on food additives or on safety requirements, as well as additional information expected by consumers. Labels have many functions: they can identify, grade, describe and promote a product.

They can describe the source of the product, its contents and principal features, how to use the product, how to care for the product, nutritional information, type and style of the product, and size and number of servings. The label can play a promotional function through the use of graphics that attract attention. The label for many products includes a machine-readable bar-code, which can be read electronically to identify the product and to produce stock and pricing information.

7.7 *Stages of the product life-cycle*

Products, like people, are viewed as having a life-cycle. Products are born, they grow, they mature, and finally they die. After a product is launched there will be times when its sales will grow and times when they will be relatively steady, and eventually it is likely that its sales will start to fall, particularly if a new product comes along that better satisfies consumers' needs, for example the decline of vinyl record sales as a result of the development of compact discs. The *product life-cycle* refers to the various stages in the life of a product, which have different marketing needs over time. A product goes through four stages in the market: introduction, growth, maturity, and decline (see fig. 7.1).

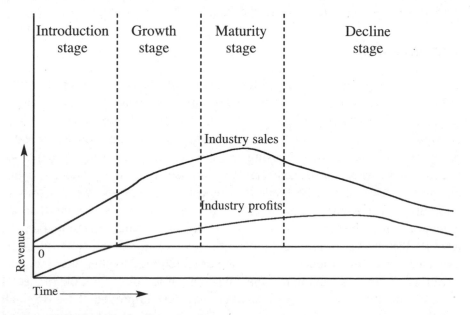

Fig. 7.1: *Stages of the product life-cycle*

Introduction stage

This is when the product is first introduced to the market. The product is new, for example digital videodisk recorders, so potential customers are likely to be wary of it and resistant to buying something new. High failure rates can result from over-optimism and lack of proper development before launching a product. It is sometimes difficult to encourage distributors to sell new products when they are concerned that the product might not reach the growth stage and that they might invest time and money in a product that would not bring them any long-term income.

At the introduction stage the product's sales grow slowly, and the profit will be small or negative, because of heavy promotion costs and production in-efficiencies. The introductory stage is a period of attempting to gain market acceptance. The marketing effort is concentrated not only on finding first-time buyers and using promotion to make them aware of the product but also on creating channels of distribution—attracting retailers and other intermediaries to handle the product. The length of the introductory stage varies dramatically; personal computers and home video games, for example, gained market acceptance rapidly. During this stage, prices can be either high or low. There-fore a company has a choice between two strategies: a *skimming strategy*, which means charging a high initial price, and a *penetration strategy*, which means charging a low price in order to discourage competitors from entering the industry. (See chapter 8 for further details on these strategies.)

Growth stage

The second stage of the product life-cycle is characterised by a rapid growth in sales and increasing profits as the product becomes better known. When the product enters its growth stage, profits can be expected to be small. As sales continue to increase during this stage, profits can be expected to increase, partly because sales are increasing but also because the start-up expenses encountered earlier can be expected to diminish. If a new product satisfies customers' needs it will be fuelled by repeat purchases and word-of-mouth publicity, and new customers are attracted to the product. A product that has entered the growth stage has shown that it may have a future in the market. As a result, the number of competitors and the level of marketing activity can be expected to increase. Pioneering firms are often required to alter their products because competitors, having had the advantage of learning from the pioneer's mistakes and the time to study the market, may have improved on the original. Products still in their growth stage include mobile phones, computerised information, and interactive shopping services.

Maturity stage

In the maturity stage the product is well known and well established, and sales begin to level off. A change in the growth rate—indicated by sales increasing at a reducing rate—heralds the end of the growth period and the beginning of the maturity stage. When the growth rate slows down, the product requires marketing strategies and tactics appropriate for the maturity stage. Later in this stage—for reasons such as diminished popularity, obsolescence, or market saturation—the product begins to lose market acceptance.

During this stage, competition is likely to be intense. Products in mature markets have solved most of the technical problems encountered early in the product's life-cycle. The products require little technical improvement, and changes become largely a matter of style. CD players, for example, are now offered in small and large sizes. They run on mains electricity, batteries, or solar power. Companies with products in mature markets whose brands are profitable typically use the funds these brands generate to support other items in the product mix. The detergent industry, for example, is in its mature stage, but the industry leader, Procter and Gamble, uses the sizeable profits generated by Tide to pay for the development and introduction of new product items and lines.

Decline stage

The product is rapidly losing market share and profitability. At this stage the marketer must decide whether it is worthwhile supporting the product for a little longer, or whether it should be discontinued. Supporting a product for which there is little natural demand is very unprofitable, but sometimes products can be revived and relaunched, perhaps in a different market. Survivor firms compete in an ever-smaller market, driving profit margins lower still. Eventually the decline stage ends with the withdrawal of the product from the market.

The assumption is that all products exhibit this life-cycle, but the time scale will vary from one product to the next. Some products—for example computer games—may go through the entire life-cycle in a matter of months.

7.8 The new-product development process

Companies need a flow of new products in order to keep their product range up to date, their customers interested, and their sales growing. Thousands of new products are developed every year in Ireland, but up to 90 per cent will fail to achieve their potential and will not survive. Failure can be expensive, particularly for a small new enterprise, which may go out of business if its only project fails.

Many factors contribute to the failure of new products; these include:

- a target market that is too small
- inadequate differentiation from existing products
- lack of access to markets because of difficulty in distribution
- poor product quality
- bad timing—launching the product too soon or too late
- poor implementation of the marketing mix.

Before describing how new products are developed, we can examine *what* a new product is. The term '***new product***' is difficult to define, as there are differing degrees of newness. This can affect how a company handles that product. The product may be new from the company's point of view or from the customer's point of view.

Newness from the company's point of view

A product may be

- new to the market (a genuine innovation, for example digital television)
- a significant innovation for the market (for example iPods)
- a minor innovation (for example blue tooth for mobile phones)
- no innovation for the market ('copycat' products).

Newness from the customer's point of view

A product may represent

- continuous innovation (for example fast-moving consumer goods, product updates, improved washing powders)
- dynamically continuous innovation (for example microchips)
- discontinuous innovation (for example mobile phones, e-mail).

7.9 *Stages in the new-product development process*

Developing and introducing new products is frequently expensive and risky. There are several stages that a product has to pass before it is ready for the market (see fig. 7.2). A company must define the role of new products in accordance with its general corporate objectives. During this stage it scans the marketing environment to identify trends that pose either opportunities or threats. Relevant company strengths and weaknesses are also identified. The outcome of this is not new-product ideas but new markets for which new products will be developed and fresh strategic roles that new products might serve. These roles help to define the direction of new-product development and to divide into externally and internally driven factors, which in turn lead to aggressive or defensive strategies.

New-product strategies can be either active, leading to an allocation of resources to identifying and seizing opportunities, or reactive, which involves taking a defensive approach, that is to say, developing copycat products.

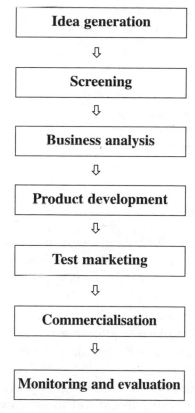

Fig. 7.2: *Stages in new-product development*

Stage 1: Idea generation

Businesses seek product ideas that will help them to achieve their objectives. In doing so they should seek to exploit their special skill or competence. The majority of companies have a structured approach to generating new-product ideas, while the source for more radical innovation is undoubtedly the individual inventor. The real difficulty companies have is not in gathering ideas but in generating successfully competitive ideas. New-product ideas come from two main sources: internal and external.

Internal sources

- marketing managers
- engineers, designers
- research and development departments
- sales representatives
- brainstorming of employees
- formal and informal suggestion schemes.

External sources

- customers' suggestions and complaints
- actual and potential competitors
- private research agencies
- distributors and suppliers
- government agencies.

Stage 2: Screening

This stage involves the preliminary assessment of ideas with a view to determining which ones should be retained. A company may use a check-list of its requirements for the development of any new product; this should include:
- an assessment of market need
- an estimate of the product life-cycle
- an estimate of competitive strengths, if any
- an estimate of the costs of launching the product.

The purpose of screening is to identify good ideas and to drop poor ideas as soon as possible. Companies should seek to avoid two types of errors in this stage. ***Drop errors*** occur when the company dismisses an otherwise good idea because of lack of vision regarding its potential. For example, IBM and Eastman Kodak (unlike Xerox) did not foresee the potential of the photocopier. If the company makes too many drop errors, its standards may be too conservative. ***Go errors*** occur when the company lets a poor idea continue on to development and commercialisation. If a company makes too many go errors, its screening criteria may not be strict enough.

Stage 3: Business analysis

The third stage involves specifying the features of the product and the marketing strategy, and making financial projections. The marketing strategy reviews the new-product idea in relation to the marketing programme needed to support it. This requires an assessment of the product idea to determine whether it will help or hinder sales of existing products. It is also examined to assess whether it can be sold through existing marketing channels or whether new outlets are needed.

Once the product's important features are defined, the company must then concentrate on the cost of research and development, and the cost of production and marketing. Regarding financial projections, the company must forecast the likely income and market share. It should carry out a break-even analysis and should estimate the return on investment to determine the profitability of the proposed product.

Stage 4: Product development

When the idea survives screening and business analysis, it moves into product development. This begins with turning the idea on paper into a sample or prototype. This involves manufacturing the product and performing laboratory and consumer tests to ensure that it meets the standards set. Many prototypes of disposable consumer goods are used and tested by consumers in their own homes; this is referred to as product testing or field testing (for example, Pepsi-Cola did this with the 'Pepsi challenge'). The product development stage seeks to determine how well the product will perform in use, and its suitability and fitness for a particular purpose.

Stage 5: Test marketing

While development and testing should reduce the risks, the stakes are now raised. As a consequence, even more care and planning is required if the product is to succeed. Many otherwise excellent products have failed because of inadequate test marketing at this stage. Test marketing must be undertaken to find out what consumers say and how they perceive the product, so that changes can be incorporated in the product before the launch.

Test marketing involves exposing actual products to potential consumers under realistic purchasing conditions to see if they will buy. Test marketing is a limited introduction of a product in areas chosen to represent the interested or target market. It is a sample launch of the entire marketing mix, and its purpose is to determine probable buyer reaction. It allows marketers to

- expose a product in its real marketing environment
- obtain a measure of sales
- correct any weaknesses before commercialisation
- vary some of the elements of the marketing mix.

There are risks with test marketing:

- it is expensive.
- it forewarns competitors.
- it can create negative bias if the wrong area is tested.

After the market tests, the company can modify the product if required, before increasing production for the full launch.

Stage 6: Commercialisation

The surviving product is now brought to the point of commercialisation, which is the full launch of the product. During this stage the company will spend large amounts of money promoting the new product. As the introduction of new products is expensive, it often involves huge risks, which may result in long delays between the development of the idea and the introduction of the product to the market. To limit these risks, companies may decide against an immediate national launch and instead have a phased introduction (a 'rolling launch'). Detailed planning and strict control will also help to minimise losses and to maximise effectiveness.

Stage 7: Monitoring and evaluation

The company must monitor the entire process so far, including the final launch of the product. Sometimes this involves setting performance criteria (volume targets) before the product is even launched. This allows forecast performance to be compared with actual performance. Any differences need to be thoroughly analysed and taken into account in the future. As we have seen, mistakes in managing the new-product development process can lead to go errors or to drop errors. At all stages in the process, therefore, the company must balance the risks involved by monitoring and evaluating the entire process.

Important terms and concepts

Case Study: New skin-friendly plaster from Elastoplast

A technologically advanced Spray Plaster launched by Elastoplast offers customers a 'one solution for all grazes and minor cuts'. It provides maximum plaster protection by forming a transparent, flexible and breathable film to seal out water, dirt and bacteria. The easy to use plaster firmly adheres to the skin without restricting joint movement. The Spray Plaster stays on for more than two days and is suitable for use on all body parts, including awkward places such as knees and elbows. The skin-friendly plaster covers the wound like a second skin to block out dirt and germs.

With forty applications in each can, the Spray Plaster has the added benefit of being waterproof, and it helps to create an optimal healing environment, allowing the wound to heal faster and effectively, without being disturbed by germs and other bacteria. Spray Plaster has become the No.1 selling Elastoplast product in Australia and has become the No.1 selling product in the first aid dressing market in Canada and France.

Source: http://www.checkout.ie/AdMarketing

Case Study: Wexford Creamery launches new cheese brand

In July 2006, Wexford Creamery launched its new cheese brand called 'Wexford Mild & Creamy Cheddar'. In maintaining its reputation for producing high-quality cheese, Wexford Creamery is supplied by 435 local farmers whose milk goes into producing this award-winning mild cheddar. All of these farmers live within a 20-mile radius of the creamery.

According to a recent *Irish Farmers Journal* National milk price audit, Wexford Creamery delivers the highest milk composition and as a result some of the best milk in Ireland. The tasty new cheddar is gentle enough in flavour for all to enjoy but with a creaminess that comes from milk produced from cattle grazing in a natural environment. This ensures that only the best milk is used to make Wexford Mild & Creamy.

Its unique packaging is very distinctive for two reasons:

- Re-closable stay fresh packs are used, ensuring that the cheese stays fresh for longer and gives the consumer extra convenience and less wastage.
- It features one of the local milk-producing farmers, Ken Chapman.

Within a few months of being introduced onto the market, Wexford Mild & Creamy has taken the Gold Medal in the Mild Category at the Wexford Organisation for Rural Development Cheese Awards 2006, won the Kerrygold Cup at the prestigious Nantwich Cheese Festival for the best Irish cheddar and taken first prize for best packaging.

Source: http://www.checkout.ie/AdMarketing

Questions for review

1. Describe the stages of new-product development.
2. Explain the concept of product life-cycle.

3. What is meant by a new product?

4. Outline the functions of packaging.

5. Explain the methods companies use to classify products.

6. Discuss and give examples of (*a*) family branding, (*b*) individual brands, (*c*) own-label brands, and (*d*) generic brands.

7. Describe the key characteristics of services.

8. Explain the term 'test marketing'.

9. How do companies generate ideas for new products?

10. What characteristics should brand names have?

8
PRICE

Chapter objectives

After reading this chapter you should be able to
- understand the meaning of price
- examine various pricing objectives
- discuss various pricing approaches
- understand pricing strategies
- identify factors influencing pricing decisions
- understand pricing in industrial markets.

8.1 *What is price?*

To a buyer, price is the value placed on what is exchanged. Page (1995) defined price as 'that which people have to forgo in order to acquire a product or service'. Simply defined, price is the amount of money charged for a product or service.

Price is stated in different terms for different exchanges; for example, a solicitor charges a *fee,* an insurance company charges a *premium,* a landlord charges *rent,* banks charge *interest.* The list of elements that can make up the true price of a purchase include:
- the stated monetary price
- taxes (for example value-added tax)
- the time required for searching, shopping, and delivery
- the delivery cost
- the installation cost
- depreciation.

Price is an important element of the marketing mix, because it relates directly to the generation of total income. A product's price is a major determinant of the market demand for a product. It affects a company's competitive position and its market share. As a result, price has a considerable bearing on a company's income and net profit. It is the only element of the marketing mix that produces income; the other three elements (product, place, and promotion) represent costs. It is only through price that money comes into a company.

So, getting the price right is a decision of fundamental importance. Much recent marketing thought has emphasised the connection between price and quality in order to defend the idea of profitable business. 'Adding value' allows a manufacturer to widen the margin of available profit by offering the consumer more benefits. Peters (1988) claims that customers, both consumer and industrial, are prepared consistently to pay more for good quality — especially if they are convinced that what they are buying is the best available. The justification for a higher price can come from any or all of the marketing mix variables:

- *Product*: offering extra features, individual specification or innovatory design.
- *Promotion*: increasing the prestige and reputation of the goods or services in question through regular advertising and promotion.
- *Price*: providing credit terms that spread payment but justify a higher eventual price.
- *Place*: guaranteeing a specific delivery date or operating hours of business that allow the customer greater convenience.

Price/Quality Relationship: Perceived product value has been described as a trade-off between the product's perceived benefits (or quality) and the perceived sacrifice – both monetary and non-monetary – necessary to acquire it. Consumers generally rely on price as an indicator of product quality. Consumers attribute different qualities to identical products that carry different price tags. Consumer characteristics such as age and income affect the perception of value. Because price is so often considered an indicator of quality, some product advertisements deliberately emphasise a high price to underscore the marketers' claims of quality. Marketers realise that, at times, products with lower prices may be interpreted as reduced quality. At the same time, when consumers evaluate more concrete attributes of a product, such as performance and durability, they rely less on the price and brand name as indicators of quality than when they evaluate the product's prestige and symbolic value. For these reasons, marketers must understand all the attributes that consumers use to evaluate a given product and include all applicable information in order to counter any perceptions of negative quality associated with a lower price.

In most situations, in addition to price, consumers also use such cues as the brand and the store in which the product is bought to evaluate its quality. In brief, consumers use price as an indicator of quality if they have little information to go on, or if they have little confidence in their own ability to make the product or service choice on other grounds. When the consumer is familiar with a brand name or has experience with a product or service or the store where it is purchased, price declines as a determining factor in product evaluation and purchase.

8.2 *Pricing objectives*

Every marketing task, including pricing, should be directed towards a goal. *Pricing objectives* are general goals that describe what a firm wants to achieve through its pricing efforts. Pricing objectives must be co-ordinated with the firm's other marketing objectives. These must, in turn, flow from the company's overall objectives. Organisational objectives could be: 'pile it high and sell it cheap', as suggested by the founder of Tesco, Sir John Cohen. More recently, however, Tesco has changed its philosophy to compete more effectively with its main competitors for the top slot in the supermarket league.

Some typical pricing objectives that companies set for themselves are:

- profit-oriented:
  — to achieve a desired return
  — to maximise profit
- sales-oriented:
  — to increase sales volume
  — to maintain or increase market share
- status-quo-oriented:
  — to stabilise prices
  — to meet competition.

Profit-oriented goals

A company may price its products to gain a certain percentage return on its sales or on its investment. This pricing policy is aimed at *achieving a target return*. Many retailers and wholesalers use a target return on net sales as a pricing objective for short periods. Target-return pricing is usually used by industry leaders, because they can set their pricing goals more independently of competition than smaller companies can.

The second profit-oriented pricing objective aims at *profit maximisation*. A profit maximisation goal is likely to be far more beneficial to a company and to the public if it is practised over a long period. To do this, however, companies sometimes have to accept short-term losses. The goal should be to maximise profits on total output rather than on each product. For example, a company might maximise total profit by setting low, relatively unprofitable prices on some products in order to stimulate sales of others, as for example with various sales promotions in supermarkets.

Sales-oriented goals

In some companies the management's pricing attention is concentrated on sales volume. The management may decide to *increase sales volume* by discounting or by some other aggressive pricing strategy, perhaps even incurring a loss in the short run.

In some companies the main pricing objective is to maintain or increase *market share*. In the late 1980s, for example, the Japanese yen rose considerably in relation to the US dollar. Companies such as Toyota, Nissan and Honda accepted smaller profit margins and reduced their costs so that they could lower their selling prices in order to maintain their market share.

Status-quo-oriented goals

Price stabilisation is often the goal of companies operating in industries where the product is highly standardised, such as steel, copper, and bulk chemicals. Status-quo objectives can have several aspects, such as maintaining a certain market share, meeting competitors' prices, or maintaining a favourable public image. One reason for seeking price stability is to avoid price wars.

8.3 Pricing strategies

Premium pricing

A premium strategy uses a high price, but gives good product/service in exchange. It is fair to customers, and, more importantly, customers see it as fair. Premium priced products could include food bought from Marks & Spencer, designer clothes or a Mercedes-Benz car.

Penetration pricing

Penetration pricing is the name given to a strategy that deliberately starts offering 'super value'. This is done to gain a foothold in the market, using price as a major weapon. It could be because other products are already well established in the market, maybe at high prices. Alternatively, penetration pricing could be used as an attempt to gain a major share of a new market. It can also deter competitors who see no profit in the market. As time goes on and the product is established, prices can be raised near market levels. Penetration pricing must be used carefully as it is very difficult to raise prices to catch up with the market levels.

Economy price

Economy pricing is a deliberate strategy of low pricing. Companies could decide to offer a 'no frills' product/service, with a price reflecting this. Before a product is launched, however, it is important to decide the position it will have in the marketplace. A product that competes purely on price is vulnerable to attack from more established products.

Price skimming

A policy of price skimming is often used for products at the introductory stage. Initially the price is pitched high, which gives a good early cash flow to offset high development costs. If the product is new, and competition has not appeared, then customers might well pay a premium to acquire a product which is offering excellent features. The launch of many home computers showed this pattern. As competitors entered the market, and new features were added by the new entrants, prices dropped for all products.

Psychological pricing

Psychological pricing is designed to get customers to respond on an emotional, rather than rational basis. It is most frequently seen in consumer markets, having less applicability in industrial markets. The most common is the use of prices such as 99 cent or €9 and 95 cent. Psychological pricing relies on the buyer's perceptions of value rather than on the seller's costs.

Product-line pricing

Product-line pricing is a strategy which involves all products offered. A supplier may decide to design a product suitable for all price levels, offering opportunities for a range of purchases. For instance, Cadbury's Time Out family bag retails for approximately, €3.82, a breakpack of nine bars €1.84, and a treat-size pack of Time Out bars at €3.08.

Pricing variations

Off-peak pricing and other special prices such as early booking discounts, stand-by prices and group discounts are used in particular circumstances. These are used in the travel trade. Stand-by prices represent a different product as there is no guarantee of travel.

8.4 *Factors influencing pricing decisions*

Price-setting can be complex, as no product is entirely without competition. There is almost always another way in which customers' needs are being satisfied, and as different customers have different needs, they will have differing views on what constitutes value for money. This is why markets need to be segmented carefully to ensure that the right price is being charged in each segment.

According to Dibb et al. (1997), most factors that affect pricing decisions can be grouped into one of the following eight categories:

Corporate and marketing objectives

Before setting a price, the company must decide on its target market and positioning strategy for the product. Marketers should set prices that are consistent with the company's goals and mission.

If the company has selected its target market and positioning carefully, then its marketing mix strategy, including price, will be relatively straightforward.

Pricing objectives

The pricing objectives are derived from the company's general objectives, for example, whether the company seeks to maximise market share or to maximise profits.

Costs

The company will want to charge a price that covers all its costs for producing, distributing and selling the product. Its costs consist of *fixed costs*, which do not vary with production or sales level, such as rent, heating, lighting, and bank interest, which have to be paid each month, regardless of the production level, and *variable costs*, which vary directly with the level of production, particularly wages, raw material costs, and energy costs. *Total costs* are the sum of the fixed and variable costs.

Other marketing mix variables

The marketer must consider the total marketing mix when setting prices. Pricing decisions can influence decisions and activities associated with product, distribution, and promotion. For example, consumers may associate a high price with better product quality, and poorer product quality with a low price. Higher-priced products, such as perfume and designer clothes, are often sold in shops such as Brown Thomas, through selective or exclusive distribution. Lower-priced products may be sold in discount shops through intensive distribution. (Distribution is discussed in more detail in chapter 9.)

Expectations of channel members

Price is also affected by the distribution channels used by a company. Channel members' costs, such as those of wholesalers and retailers, must also be met.

Buyer perceptions

Members of one market segment may be more sensitive to price than members of a different target market. Marketers must try to ascertain a consumer's reasons for buying the product and must set the price according to consumers' perceptions of the product's value. Buyers' perceptions of a product, relative to competing products, may allow a company to set a price that differs significantly from the price of competing products. If the product is considered superior to most of the competition, a company may charge a higher price for its product.

Competition

A marketer will need to know the prices competitors charge at present and will also have to take into account the possible entry of new competitors. Prices may be set higher than those of competitors in order to give an impression of exclusivity or higher quality. This is common practice in beauty salons and restaurants.

Legal and regulatory issues

Governments, through legislation to protect consumers, may influence pricing decisions, for example, price controls may be introduced to curb inflation.

8.5 *Managing price changes*

Prices are rarely static for long periods. Competitive pressures may force prices down, either temporarily or permanently, or new market opportunities might increase the price premium on a product. Changing prices, however, can have a serious effect on profit margins and on market stability. Normally, it is likely that a price cut will increase the volume of sales, and it is sometimes a very fine calculation to predict whether the profit margin earned on the extra volume gained more than compensates for the lost margin caused by the price cut. At various times, a company may be faced with the prospect of initiating price changes, or of responding to competitors' price changes.

Initiating price cuts can be a dangerous activity. Nevertheless, companies still cut prices from time to time. They may do so for short-term tactical reasons, such as clearing excess stock, or as part of a more fundamental strategic 'value for money' repositioning. Much depends on whether the company sees itself as a price leader or follower in the market. A market leader may wish to make the first move, leaving competitors with the problem of whether to respond, and how.

On the other hand, when a company is faced with a competitor's price rise, it has to decide whether and how to respond. There are three possible responses:

- Respond in kind by matching the competitor's move.
- Maintain price levels, but differentiate the product by emphasising how much better value it now represents.
- Or refuse to respond at all.

Many companies prefer to follow others in implementing price rises, rather than taking the leadership risks. Smaller companies may use the leader's price as a reference point, follow the price and continue to compete on non-price factors such as location, service and adaptability. Promoting further differentiation may be the best option for defending a niche.

Not responding at all is perhaps the highest-risk option, if it is perceived as an aggressive response designed to gain market share. Smaller companies may have more flexibility in their response, as their actions are likely to have only a marginal impact. The specific response selected will primarily depend on how much the other organisations in the market want market stability and to shelter under the price umbrella created by the price leader.

8.6 *General pricing approaches*

Marketers need to decide what price will be regarded by customers as good value for money, while still allowing the company to make a profit. The main methods of pricing used by companies are cost-based, customer-based, and competition-based.

Cost-based pricing

Two cost-based pricing methods are ***cost-plus pricing*** and ***mark-up pricing***. *Cost-plus* pricing involves calculating all the costs of making a product (including production, promotion, distribution, and overheads) and adding an amount to provide an acceptable level of profit.

Item	Cost per unit
	€
Labour costs	3.50
Raw materials	5.30
Overheads	4.20
Promotion	2.50
Distribution	1.40
Total production cost per unit	16.90
Add profit of 20%	*3.38*
Net price	**20.28**

Table 8.1: *An example of cost-plus pricing*

This method, however, does not take account of how customers will react to the quoted prices. If they perceive that the price does not represent value for money, they will not buy the product. Alternatively, if they perceive that the price is exceptionally good value for money, the company may not have enough stock to meet the demand, and competitors will be able to enter the market easily.

Mark-up pricing

Mark-up pricing is similar to cost-plus pricing and is the method used by most retailers. A retailer will buy in stock and add on a fixed percentage to the bought-in price (a mark-up) in order to arrive at the shelf price. Usually there is a standard mark-up for each product category. In some cases the mark-up will be 100 per cent or more, while in other cases it will be close to nil if the retailer believes that stocking the product will stimulate other sales.

According to Kotler and Armstrong (1990), some common mark-ups in supermarkets are 9 per cent on baby foods, 14 per cent on tobacco products, 20 per cent on bakery products, 27 per cent on dried foods and vegetables, 37 per cent on spices and extracts, and 50 per cent on greeting cards.

	€
Bought-in price	2.00
Mark-up at 25%	.50
Shelf price	2.50

Table 8.2: *An example of mark-up pricing*

Mark-up pricing is a popular approach, because sellers are more certain about costs than about demand. As the price is tied to cost, sellers do not have to make frequent adjustments to price as demand changes.

When all firms in the industry use this pricing method, prices tend to be similar, and price competition is reduced. A disadvantage, however, is that any pricing method that ignores environmental demand and competition is not likely to lead to the best pricing structure.

Customer-based pricing

Two customer-based pricing methods are demand-based pricing and psychological pricing. Marketers sometimes use demand-based pricing rather than establishing the price of a product on its costs. *Demand-based pricing* is determined by the level of demand for the product, resulting in a high price when demand is strong and a low price when demand is weak. Demand-based pricing usually begins with the marketer assessing what the demand will be for the product at varying prices. This is usually done by asking customers what they might expect to pay for the product, and seeing how many choose each price level. Table 8.3 shows the development of demand-based pricing:

Price per unit	Number of customers who said they would buy at this price
€10–11	20,000
€11–12	15,000
€12–13	10,000
€13–14	5,000

Table 8.3: *Assessment of customer reaction for demand pricing*

As the price rises, fewer customers are prepared to buy the product, as fewer will then see the product as good value for money.

The next stage in demand pricing is calculating the costs of producing the commodity, as the cost of producing each item usually falls as more are made. To use this method, a marketer must be able to estimate the quantity of a product that customers will demand at different prices. The marketer then chooses the price that generates the highest total income. The effectiveness of this method depends on the marketer's ability to estimate demand accurately. *Psychological pricing* involves both prestige pricing and odd-even pricing.

Higher prices are often used as an indicator of quality, so some companies will use *prestige pricing*. This method is used especially when buyers associate a higher price with higher quality. Prestige pricing is used for luxury items, such as perfumes, jewellery, and clothes. Service industries, such as restaurants and hotels, often use psychological pricing because of the value added by atmosphere and service. Companies use the non-price marketing-mix variables to build up perceived value, in customers' minds. Price is set to match the perceived value, for example, customers expect to pay more for a cup of coffee at a five-star hotel than at a McDonald's restaurant.

Odd-even pricing is a method of psychological pricing suggesting that buyers are influenced by prices ending in different digits. Odd pricing assumes that more of a product will be sold at €9.99 than €10. Odd pricing refers to a price ending in 1, 3, 5, 7, 9, just under a round number (e.g. €0.79, €2.97, €34.95). Even pricing refers to a price ending in a whole number or in tenths (e.g. €0.50, €6.10, €55.00).

Competition-based pricing

Competition-based pricing recognises the influence of competition in the market. The marketer must decide how close the competition is in providing for customers' needs. If the products are similar, prices will need to be similar to those of the competition. This method is important if a company is serving markets in which price is the main variable of the marketing strategy.

Companies with large market share often have enough control within their industries to become price leaders. Smaller firms tend to follow the price fluctuations of the leading brands rather than basing price on demand for their own product changes or when cost changes.

8.7 *The influence of the product life-cycle on pricing decisions*

As we saw in chapter 7, a product passes through various stages during its life-cycle. When a new product reaches the market, a company has to choose between various strategies in determining a price for its product.

Pricing during the introduction phase

Dean (1950) first identified three objectives that all companies share when pricing a new product:

- to establish the product in the market
- to maintain market share in the face of competition from later entrants
- to produce profits.

During this phase a company may choose pioneer pricing, market-penetration pricing, or market-skimming pricing. *Pioneer pricing* involves setting a base price for a new product. This can be set high to recover research and development costs quickly or to provide a reference point for developing discount prices for different market segments. Marketers need to consider how quickly competitors will enter the market when setting base prices. If competitors can enter the market easily and quickly, the first company may adopt a base price that will discourage competitors.

Market-penetration pricing is used when a company sets a low price for a new product in order to attract a large number of buyers and a large market share. This strategy can also be used to undercut higher-priced products that are already established in the market. As time passes and the product becomes established, prices can be raised nearer market levels. Alternatively, supplier costs could fall as volume increases. In this case the consumer benefits from a continuation of the low prices. Market-penetration pricing, however, must be used carefully, as it is very difficult to restore prices to market levels.

Market-skimming pricing is the practice of starting out with a high price for a new product, then reducing the price as sales level off. A policy of price skimming is often used for products at the introductory stage of the product life-cycle. If the product is new and competition has not appeared, customers might be willing to pay a higher price to acquire a product that is offering excellent features. The launch of many home computers and video recorders showed this pattern, as competitors came into the market and new features were added by new entrants, resulting in falling prices for these products.

If companies choose to use market-skimming pricing, product quality and image must support the higher price, and enough customers must want the product at that price. Additionally, competitors should not be able to enter the market easily and undercut the high price.

Pricing during the growth phase

Pricing strategy during the growth phase of the product life-cycle will be influenced by the choice that was made at the introductory phase between skimming and penetration strategies. For marketers who followed the skimming strategy, prices will probably need to fall during the growth phase. The reason for this might be the arrival of more competition. For marketers who followed a market-penetration strategy, the growth phase represents the best opportunity to increase prices. This is because the market is now growing in size, and even with the arrival of additional competitors there may still be enough demand to justify price increases.

Prices during the maturity phase

As demand peaks, the pressure between companies supplying the same market increases. One way in which a company can achieve sales growth is by means of price reductions, with the aim of driving the least-efficient competitors out of the market. This, however, can lead to risky or damaging price wars.

Prices during the decline phase

Prices and profitability can be expected to fall during the decline stage, as the perceived differences between brands are likely to be insignificant and there are usually only very limited opportunities to reduce costs. The fact that a product has now fully repaid its development and investment costs may still make its production and marketing profitable.

8.8 *Pricing in industrial markets*

Industrial products can be those purchased for resale, or they can be raw materials which are incorporated into manufactured products, or consumables used in industrial operations (see Chapter 2). Consumables are the convenience goods of the industrial market, however, there is no need for fancy packaging to attract shoppers as in a supermarket. They therefore tend to have basic packaging for protection, and can often be supplied in multiple packs. The price will reflect this. In addition, there may be a quantity discount. Business is usually done on credit and it is common to offer discounts to customers who pay their invoice within a specified number of days. There is no role for psychological pricing, but it is common for the sales negotiators to be given some freedom in the price to be charged.

Raw materials will be regular purchases, and it is probably more important that suppliers are reliable. Customers will be prepared to pay a little extra to a known, and trusted, supplier rather than risk supply problems. A customer, however, may operate a policy of sourcing from a number of suppliers in order to compare competition prices. If the supplier builds up a strong relationship with the customer, then a good exchange of information takes place, and prices are continually discussed along with other issues. There may be an annual contract between supplier and customer which confirms price for the whole year. The above pricing methods are possible because industrial markets have much more direct contact between supplier and customer through the wide use of direct personal selling in these markets.

There is one difficult area of industrial market, however, where direct selling is not a factor. This is when suppliers are invited to submit a tender for a contract offered by a large customer, who may be a local authority or a government department. In this situation the customer specifies what they want, and asks a number of suppliers to submit a bid. In such a case it is necessary not only to carry out detailed costing on what is required, but also to have an appreciation of who else is bidding for the work. Here, a pricing strategy can be based on the knowledge of the competition, as well as how badly an organisation wants the contract. The final price is therefore a marketing decision, and not based solely on costs.

Important terms and concepts

price: p. 122
pricing objectives: p. 124
profit-oriented goals: p. 124
target return: p. 124
profit maximisation: p. 124
sales-oriented goals: p. 125
status-quo-oriented goals: p. 125
premium pricing: p. 125
penetration pricing: p. 125
economy price: p. 126
price skimming: p. 126

product-line pricing: p. 126
pricing variations: p. 127
factors influencing pricing decisions:
    p. 127
corporate and marketing objectives:
    p. 127
pricing objectives: p. 127
fixed costs: p. 127
variable costs: p. 127
total costs: p. 127
general pricing approaches: p. 130

Case Study: Tesco: 'Better, Simpler, Cheaper'

The Tesco store at Dundrum Town Centre has been one of the strongest performing in the group's network. Store manager, Pat Stapleton believes in the policy 'Better, Simpler, Cheaper'. The store brings in 38,000 transactions per week, and trade sources suggest that while other stores in Dundrum may have struggled to live up to the hype, the Tesco store 'is a crown jewel, not a white elephant'.

According to Stapleton, the success of the trade is being driven by three key factors: range, availability and value. Tesco Dundrum carries up to 40,000 lines at any one time, with the sheer size of the store allowing for a much larger range of Tesco own-brand products than many of the former Quinnsworth stores, particularly in the area of fresh food products. These along with health and beauty, have been the hero categories for Dundrum.

The core shopper at Dundrum has remained the same in the last six months, with the average shopper visiting the store between 5p.m. and 10p.m., and shopping for non-food, meat and fresh produce through to health and beauty and finally onto the main thoroughfare of the store – the central artery which links all the grocery aisles. The central aisle is one of the principal selling features of the store, both due to its size and the large amount of promotions it facilitates. Each end features one major promotion, for example, '3 for 2' or some other value promotion. This may not be unusual for a large supermarket, but what Tesco Dundrum has that many other large stores does not is the space and capacity to ensure that not only are customers aware of the promotion, there are no out-of-stocks after a busy Friday night or Saturday afternoon. Eliminating out-of-stocks is a key focus for all Tesco stores, an ethos which has clearly filtered down to store level in Dundrum. Stapleton firmly believes that for all Tesco's heavy price discounting and special offers, the real key to customer retention and satisfaction is ensuring that out-of-stocks do not occur.

Stapleton suggests that 'running a store that never closes is a different challenge but it has so many advantages. We can merchandise 95% of our stock at night, which means that the customers get what they want and when they want it. Our motto is that customers should always get what they want, and they can do so with clear aisles and they do not have to queue, and that's what we live and die for'.

Like most industry watchers, Stapleton recognises the potential that Tesco has for Ireland, and is confident that it has the right tools both to expand in terms of store numbers and improve in-store offers. Analysis of customer trends means that Tesco is now 'disappointing customers less and less'. As Stapleton says 'We've always got to be looking ahead, we've got to be looking at how to make things better, we've done a lot but we have to be different, we've got to be simpler, we've got to be more innovative, we've got to be cheaper and we've got to be better. Simpler, cheaper, better, that's the key'.

Source http://www.checkout.ie

Case Study: The Pigsback.com

Pigsback.com is the 'brand' of Empathy Marketing Limited, a company set up in 2000 with the idea of bringing 'brands and consumers together for mutual benefit'. Pigsback.com has become one of Ireland's most visited websites, with over 6.5 million impressions every month and over 25,000 unique visitors per day. Pigsback.com provides a gateway for consumers to make savings when purchasing anything from CDs to flights, or by taking part in surveys (such as consumer intelligence), and basically rewarding the consumer for shopping and time. By purchasing products and services from companies through Pigsback.com, members earn 'PiggyPoints', which have a value of one cent each. These can be redeemed for a host of different rewards, including Xtra-vision vouchers, CDs and cinema tickets.

Consumers are also encouraged to visit and return to Pigsback.com because every offer that appears on the site is exclusive to Pigsback.com. According to the company, the most popular sections include grocery coupons, hotel offers and Xtra-Vision vouchers. According to CEO, Michael Dwyer, Pigsback.com is an 'ideal solution' for Irish companies as a result of the high numbers of visitors to the site. With 200,000 members to target, Pigsback supports the overall media mix of brand marketing campaigns by acting as the interactive hub in the mix. This reflects the overall above-the-line campaign, and adds the benefit of proactive interactions with the brand (in the form of coupon prints, competition entries, polls, etc.) as opposed to the general branding/awareness of a traditional media mix. On Pigsback.com, brands are promoted in a number of ways, including through sponsorship of zones, feature promotions, interactive advertising, competitions, coupon programmes, and product sampling offers. The site now has over 250 different offers from more than 150 brands, with over seven million coupons for brands such as Kellogg's, Dove and Goodfella's printed to date.

Of these promotions, couponing has become one of the most popular and successful, according to Pigsback.com marketing director Gareth Lambe. 'By running a coupon programme on Pigsback.com, brands not only get a sustained marketing presence online but also quality interactions with the consumer. A brand can expect 40-50,000 prints of their coupon from the site over six months, with an average redemption rate of 20% – with some brands getting as high as 40%. Pigsback follow up with surveys to the redeemers of the coupons, giving the brands valuable and quick feedback from the consumer'. It is this feedback and relationship between Pigsback.com and its members that has made it so popular both with advertisers, partners and consumers, and as such makes it the ideal vehicle for Consumer Intelligence.

Although the relationship between Pigsback.com and its members is fundamentally based on exclusive offers, rewards, and ultimately price savings for the consumer, it is also a core principle of 'permission based marketing', which means that the member's permission must be obtained before they are communicated to in any way. According to Pigsback.com, this principle allows members to feel they are in control, and ensures that they trust the Pigsback.com brand. When a member signs up with Pigsback.com they indicate their categories of interest and from that information their personalised home page is built. In this way, it is highly targeted and the member is in total control. If members want they can sign up for emails, but they are never sent an email unless they specifically ask to be communicated with in this way. These communications include 'Curly's Grocery Coupons', (105,000 subscribers) a fortnightly email which offers coupons, which can be printed and savings of up to €25 per week can be made.

Source: http://www.checkout.ie

Questions for review

1. What are the main factors that influence pricing decisions for a company?
2. Outline the various approaches to pricing products.
3. What are the pricing objectives a marketer considers when setting prices?
4. Discuss the influence of the product life-cycle on pricing decisions.
5. Explain (*a*) demand-based pricing and (*b*) psychological pricing. Illustrate your answer with examples.
6. Outline some of the pricing strategies a marketing manager may choose from.
7. Discuss pricing in industrial markets.

9
DISTRIBUTION

Chapter objectives

After reading this chapter you should be able to
- understand the role of distribution in marketing
- discuss the aspects of physical distribution and distribution channels
- compare direct distribution with intermediary distribution
- examine the functions of distribution channels.

9.1 *Distribution in the marketing mix*

Distribution is the process by which goods or services are made available and accessible to consumers. In terms of the 'four Ps', distribution is the means by which *place* is determined. Marketers, therefore, expend considerable effort on finding the right *channels of distribution* to ensure that their products reach customers in the most efficient way. According to Dibb et al. (1997), 'a channel of distribution (or marketing channel) is a group of individuals and organisations that direct the flow of products from producers to customers.'

The main concerns for marketers in establishing a distribution network are:

- timing—will the product be available when the market expects it?
- location—will the product be in the places where consumers expect to find it?
- reliability—will the distribution system deliver what it promised, or will the retailer be apologising to consumers for delays?

The purpose of any physical distribution method is to transfer the product from its point of production to the consumer in as efficient and effective a way as possible. A company's ability to satisfy consumers' needs efficiently and effectively depends on its relationships with its own suppliers. The product must arrive in good condition and must fit the target market's needs for convenience, or choice, or whatever else the particular segment thinks is important. Late, damaged, incorrect or inefficiently small deliveries and unsold products show a lack of proper management of the distribution process. During the late 1980s serious delivery problems with the Adidas range of sports footwear gave Reebok and Nike their chance to increase their share of the European market.

9.2 *Distribution channels*

Distribution channel decisions are among the most important facing managers. A company's channel decisions directly affect every other marketing decision. The company's pricing depends on whether it uses mass merchandising or high-quality specialty stores. Distribution channels manage the series of exchanges that a product or service goes through as it is transferred from its producer to its final user. Channels can be constructed of a number of go-betweens or none at all, as in the case of direct marketing. The main aim of any marketing decision relating to distribution channels is how to reach the relevant customers. This must be in the most appropriate way, given the following four major considerations:

Customers' requirements

The choice of efficient distribution channels relies on a knowledge of a particular market, and in particular it relies on the needs and wants of customers. It may not be possible to satisfy everything a particular customer wants, but that customer's decision is likely to be based on issues such as cost, availability and convenience. The decision facing potential customers is how they rate the different elements of cost and convenience. Opening times are relevant to the availability decision of customers, for example, a neighbourhood store, managed by the owner, is likely to be open for longer hours than a supermarket in an out-of-town shopping centre. The local store will have a limited choice and is likely to be slightly more expensive, but travel time to the supermarket and queues at the checkout at a peak period must be considered.

Organisational resources

The choice of channels has to be consistent with the needs and capabilities of the organisation as well as meeting the needs of customers. An organisation will normally make decisions on the market segments to which they want to offer their product first. Many companies admit they are better off working through intermediaries because they can provide the resources to cover all the potential customers in a cost-effective way, for example, food manufacturers market via retailers rather than directly. One problem arising from the use of intermediaries is that it almost invariably leads to some loss of control over the way markets are served.

Competitors' and distributors' actions

Control of the distribution channel is a very effective barrier to entry in many markets. Even if it is possible to gain access to a general distributor alongside competitive products, it will not be enough if the distributor constantly recommends a competitor's product.

Legal constraints

The legal environment is important as there are issues such as product liability laws which affect all offerings. These restrictions vary from country to country. Key legislation such as the Sale of Goods Act puts responsibilities on retailers. Policies on returned stock, and replacing faulty goods, are a key element of distribution policy and customer service.

9.3 *Physical distribution and logistics*

Physical distribution refers to the broad range of activities concerned with the efficient movement of finished products from the end of the production line to the consumer. Physical distribution is concerned with transport methods, and distribution strategy decisions are concerned with the choice of outlets for the product. Physical distribution has many objectives. According to Zikmund and d'Amico (1996), these objectives can be condensed into one general statement of purpose: to minimise cost while maximising customer service. Companies can establish competitive advantages over their competitors by more effective physical distribution. Providing more reliable or faster delivery, avoiding errors in processing orders and delivering undamaged goods are all potential competitive advantages.

Logistics refers to the entire process of moving raw materials and component parts into the firm, products in process through the firm, and finished goods out of the firm. The term includes both materials management and physical distribution of the final product; logistics management therefore involves planning, implementing and controlling both the efficient inward flow of materials and the outward flow of finished products. Logistics involves strategic decision-making about the location of warehouses, the management of materials, stock levels, and information systems.

9.4 *Aspects of physical distribution*

Physical distribution involves planning, implementing, and controlling the physical flow of materials and final goods from points of origin to points of use in order to meet the needs of customers at a profit. The major physical distribution cost is transportation, followed by inventory carrying, warehousing, and order processing/customer service. Physical distribution, however, is more than a cost – it can help create demand. Companies can attract more customers by giving better service or lower prices through better physical distribution. On the other hand, companies lose customers when they fail to supply goods on time.

Many companies state their objective as getting the right goods to the right places at the right time for the least cost. Unfortunately, no physical distribution system can *both* maximise customer service *and* minimise distribution costs. The process of physical distribution can be looked at as a system. The main functions carried out by a physical distribution system are:

Order processing

This first stage in a distribution system is a crucial one from the marketing point of view. It involves contact with the customer and offers an opportunity to introduce service advantages over the competition. The system design should include speed, ease of use and efficiency.

Materials handling

Often the physical attributes of a product, for example, perishability, weight and bulk will be the decisive influence in how it is stored and transported. Balancing service levels and cost means working out the most efficient use of warehouse space, which will affect the shape, size and nature of the packaging used.

Warehousing

The geographical location of warehouses relative to production and consumption location is a key consideration for manufacturers. A company must decide on how many and what types of warehouses it needs. The more warehouses a company uses, the more quickly goods can be delivered to customers and the higher the service level. More locations, however, mean higher warehousing costs. A company must, therefore, balance the level of customer service against distribution costs. A company might own private warehouses, rent space in public warehouses or both. They may use storage warehouses or distribution centres. **Storage warehouses** store goods for moderate to long periods, whereas **distribution centres** are designed to move goods rather than just store them. A distribution centre is a large computerised centre designed to receive goods from various companies and suppliers, take orders, fill them efficiently and deliver goods to customers as quickly as possible. In a distribution centre, the emphasis is on throughput.

Inventory management

Adequate stocks of working materials are vital, but too much money tied up in this way can mean cash-flow disaster. Carrying too little may result in costly emergency shipments, customer dissatisfaction or lost sales as unserved customers move to a competitor. Inventory decisions involve knowing both when to order and how much to order. On average, stock will account for between a third and a half of the assets of most businesses. Careful thought must be given to how much to reorder and at what intervals. Typically the cost of storage averages out at about 25% of the stock's value per year.

Just-in-time

In recent years many companies have greatly reduced their inventories and related costs through *just-in-time* (JIT) logistics systems. JIT aims at maximising the efficiency of the manufacturing process by carrying the minimum level of stock necessary. New stock arrives at the factory or retail outlet exactly when needed, rather than being stored in inventory until being used. JIT systems require accurate forecasting along with fast, frequent and flexible delivery, so that new supplies will be available when needed. These systems result in substantial savings in inventory carrying and handling costs. By keeping the flow in the pipeline — raw materials, work-in-progress, finished goods — to a minimum, suppliers can enhance logistics efficiency, while ensuring that customer service objectives are regularly met.

Transport

The final aspect of physical distribution is the transport which moves the product from where it is produced to where it is used. It is one of the most frequently contracted-out aspects of distribution, although many major manufacturers will maintain their own fleets of haulage vehicles (see section 9.5).

9.5 *Transport methods*

Transport is the process of moving a product from where it is made to where it is bought. Methods of transport vary according to speed, cost, and ability to handle the type of product concerned. The principal transport infrastructures are railways, roads, airways, water transport, and pipelines. Each mode offers advantages and disadvantages, and the distribution manager or transport manager must therefore consider the cost trade-offs involved in selecting one of the modes of transport. The first consideration is always the needs of the customer. Other considerations include the nature of the product, for example bulk, perishability, weight, and fragility, and the cost and availability of transport methods and storage space.

Railways carry heavy, bulky goods over long distances at low cost. Railways often carry minerals, sand, timber and chemicals as well as low-value manufactured goods. The main disadvantages of the railway system are that it is relatively slow and it can be used only near railway lines. Some companies, however, establish their factories or warehouses near rail lines for convenient loading and unloading.

Motor vehicles include lorries, vans and, to a lesser extent, buses that carry packages. Lorries are the most flexible and accessible mode of transport, as they can go almost anywhere. They are often used in conjunction with forms of transport that cannot provide door-to-door delivery. Motor vehicles and their services, however, can be expensive. Lorries are most efficient at moving comparatively small deliveries over short distances, and are also effective for long distances.

Air freight is the fastest but also the most expensive mode of distribution. The primary advantages of air freight are its speed and its distance capabilities. Fast transport also permits stock reductions and savings in warehousing costs. Air transport is used primarily to move goods of high unit value, perishable goods, and emergency orders. High-technology manufacturers often choose to move goods on demand by air freight rather than incur the costs of carrying stock. The ground transport needed for pick-up and final delivery, however, also adds to cost and transit time.

Water transport usually offers a very low-cost means of moving products. It is most appropriate for bulky, low-value, non-perishable goods, such as grain and coal. Many markets, however, are accessible to water only with supplementary rail or road transport. The main disadvantages of water transport are its slowness and the seasonal closing of some routes and ports by ice during winter.

Pipelines are the most specialised means of transport, because they are designed to carry only one or two products. They are used mainly to transport natural gas and crude petroleum, moving them from wells to storage or treatment facilities. Most pipelines are owned by the companies that use them, such as gas and oil producers. Pipelines move products slowly but continuously and at relatively low cost. They are a reliable mode of transport and ensure low rates of product damage and theft. A large part of the expense results from the construction of the pipeline itself.

Marketers select a transport mode on the grounds of cost, speed, reliability, capability, accessibility, security, and traceability. They compare alternative means of transport to determine whether the benefits from a more expensive mode are worth the higher costs. The cheapest is not always the best, for example, microchips are light and therefore relatively cheap in air freight charges, without tying up capital in lengthy surface routes.

Marketers also compare **transit time**, which is the total time for transporting products, including the time required for pick-up and delivery, handling, and movement between the points of manufacture and destination. The **reliability** of a mode of transport is determined by the consistency of service provided. Marketers must be able to know that their products will be delivered on time and in an acceptable condition. **Capability** refers to the provision of appropriate equipment and conditions for moving specific products, for example refrigeration. **Accessibility** is the carrier's capacity to move products over a specific route or network, for example railway lines, water-ways, or roads. **Security** means delivering the products in an acceptable condition, for example not losing or damaging the goods. Highly valuable items, for example, may not be easily distributed through retailers, as direct delivery may work better. **Traceability** is the means of finding products that have been lost.

9.6 *Who does what in distribution?*

Channel intermediaries fall into two main types: merchants and functional intermediaries. Merchant's actually become the legal owners of the goods they then resell. The risks are substantial because if the goods do not sell it becomes the merchant's problem. However, the potential profit to be made is correspondingly higher than being an agent or functional intermediary.

Functional intermediaries never actually own the goods that pass through their hands. They earn a commission or fee for the services they provide. These can include transport, storage and finance. The following are the main sorts of distribution intermediaries:

Agent

A functional intermediary with a contractual agreement to work on behalf of a particular buyer or seller. Agents find customers and negotiate, but never actually own the goods in question. They receive a fee or commission for their work.

Broker

Similar to an agent, but with fewer functions. These are mainly limited to bringing together buyers and sellers. They are employed temporarily and paid by the parties hiring them. The most familiar examples are insurance brokers, auctioneering brokers and security brokers.

Cash and carry

A type of wholesaler whose customers are not offered credit and have to collect their purchases themselves. Smaller independent retailers will often use a cash and carry (e.g. Musgraves) in conjunction with traditional full-service wholesalers and company sales representatives in order to deal with their stocking needs.

Facilitator

Firms like hauliers, warehouses, banks and insurance companies help expedite exchanges without owning the goods concerned.

Franchisee

An individual or an organisation granted the exclusive right to exploit a successful business idea by its originator (franchisor) in return for profit, for example, Tie Rack, Sock Shop and Body Shop.

Franchisor

The owner of a successful business idea who franchises it out to a number of franchisees.

In-home retailers

Companies that sell direct in people's homes rather than using traditional retail environments, for example, Avon or Tupperware.

9.7 Marketing intermediaries

One of the major decisions facing a manufacturer is whether to sell directly to consumers or to use intermediaries, or both. Fig. 9.1 summarises the strengths and weaknesses of direct versus intermediary distribution methods. A *direct-marketing channel* has no intermediary levels: for example, the Book Club of

Ireland, Family Album and Viking Direct (office supplies) sell their products by mail order, while others, for example Amazon, sell goods through the world wide web. It includes mail order, free phone numbers, and marketing on the Internet. Direct marketing is now becoming more widely used because of increased use of the Internet and credit card payments.

Direct channels	**Intermediary channels**
Manufacturer	Manufacturer
⇩	⇩
Consumer	Middleman
	⇩
	Consumer

Fig. 9.1: *Direct and intermediary distribution channels*

Most, though not all, channels of distribution have **marketing intermediaries**. An intermediary or 'middleman' is an independent business concern that operates as a link between producers and consumers or industrial users. **Agents** do not actually buy products, but agency sales representatives call on major retailers and on wholesalers on behalf of a number of producers, and take orders and arrange delivery. This saves the producer the cost of operating a large sales force to carry perhaps only a small product range, enlisting instead, for example, insurance brokers and recruitment agencies. Agents are usually paid a fee or commission for their work. **Wholesalers** buy the goods from the manufacturers, often through an agent, then sell the goods to retailers, for example Musgrave (Super Valu and Centra). **Retailers** are companies that offer goods directly to consumers, for example local shops and supermarkets.

Direct	**Intermediaries**
• enables companies to build strong relationships with consumers	• buy more per order than individual consumers
• puts the distribution network under the control of the manufacturer	• are physically closer to consumers and can provide market information
• increases margins on sales by cutting out the mark-up of intermediaries	• can offer after-sales service in places convenient to consumers, rather than returning products to a factory for service

Fig. 9.2: *Direct versus intermediary distribution*

9.8 *Internet marketing*

The potential audience for Internet usage is very large, as more and more homes and businesses either get connected or develop their own websites. Mitchell (1999) argues that the Internet has revolutionised the way in which transactions are done and can reduce interaction costs, both of which are critical aspects of exchange, whether for profit or some other benefit. If sales, marketing and distribution account for around 30% of the cost of a product, then the Internet could reduce them to 20%, with some of those savings passed on to the customer through lower prices.

Despite the significant impact of the Internet, the difficulty for marketers is the technology driving website use. Speeds can still be relatively slow when traffic levels are high. As the number of people logging on to the Internet increases, the problem will become more severe unless bandwidth and capacity problems are resolved.

There are, however, several advantages of on-line distribution that conventional mail order cannot achieve:

- The user is actively searching for products and services, and so every site hit could gain a potential customer if interest can be maintained.
- Print and mailing costs are eliminated because no catalogue has to be produced and distributed each season.
- Order processing and handling costs are reduced with on-line ordering as everything is already in electronic form and the customer is handling all the order entry without assistance.

9.9 *Distribution strategies*

Companies have to choose the optimum number of middlemen to use. Determining the number of wholesalers and the number of retailers is an important decision, which will determine the number of outlets where potential customers can expect to find the product. There are three levels of distribution: intensive, selective, and exclusive.

Intensive distribution seeks to obtain maximum exposure for the product at the retail level. When consumers will not go to much effort to buy a product, or will readily accept substitutes when the brand is not available, the appropriate strategy is to use all available outlets for distributing a product. The goods must be available where and when customers want them. Intensive distribution at the wholesale level allows almost all appropriate wholesalers to carry the product. Coca-Cola, for example, is distributed in vending machines, supermarkets, convenience stores, restaurants, and many other outlets. Cigarettes, bread and newspapers are also intensively distributed.

Selective distribution at the retail level restricts the sale of the product to a limited number of outlets. Each selected shop must meet the company's performance standards while appealing to a select target market. Selective distribution is more commonly used for speciality goods, for example, with electrical appliances and photographic specialists, who can offer professional advice; and exclusive perfumes usually fall into the specialist category, rather than convenience goods. This type of restricted distribution, however, is becoming less common, with supermarkets, pharmacies and department stores offering increasingly wider ranges of household and electrical goods.

Exclusive distribution uses only one outlet in a particular area to sell a product. When a product requires personal selling, a complete stock of the product line, repair service, or other special effort, an intermediary may be granted exclusive distribution rights. Exclusive distribution is suitable for products that are bought rather infrequently, are consumed over a long period, or require information to fit them to consumers' needs. It is often used as an incentive to sellers when only a limited market is available for products. Cars such as Rolls-Royce and watches such as Rolex are sold on an exclusive basis. Generally a manufacturer or wholesaler that grants a retailer exclusive distribution expects a maximum sales effort, or expects to gain something from the prestige or efficiency of the retail outlet.

9.10 *Distribution and the product life-cycle*

As with other aspects of the marketing mix, product and service distribution objectives will differ from phase to phase in the product's life-cycle. During the introduction phase it is vital for a manufacturer to have secured an effective distribution network by the time the product is launched. If the new product is joining a company's existing range of branded products, this should not be too difficult, as the existing channels are likely to be suitable for the new product. Wholesalers and retailers, however, will expect incentives to stock a new brand, in the form of discounted prices and merchandising support.

During the growth phase, wholesalers and retailers will be more likely to stock the product, as demand will be growing and intermediaries will want to be able to satisfy this. At the maturity phase, both the retailer and the manufacturer of a brand may review their strategies, for example retailers may want to decrease the number of competing brands in a product group to concentrate on best-sellers, while manufacturers may want to concentrate distribution through the most cost-effective outlets, eliminating those that take only small orders. During the decline phase, manufacturers face pressure from retailers to offer bigger discounts just to keep the brand on the shelves.

9.11 *Getting products into distribution: the push-pull methods*

There are two methods by which products get into a distribution channel. The first is through the efforts of a sales team to convince distributors to stock the product. This involves *pushing* products into the distribution channel. A good salesperson will not overload distributors with products but will try to make sure the right level of product is available to meet customers' requirements. Push tactics can be seen to be a sales-led approach, with salespersons offering special discounts, sale or return, merchandising support, and dealer competitions. The use of bar-codes means that sales can be tracked efficiently, and in some cases the reordering of products is assisted by automation.

Pull tactics are advertising-led. Consumers can create demand, pulling products along a distribution chain, for example, by ordering the product, demand pull is created. Before this can be achieved, however, awareness of the product needs to be promoted, for example through advertising or through informal recommendations. Push and pull tactics can operate quite independently of each other but work best if combined. In practice, most markets have a mixture of push and pull techniques. Both tactics are necessary to keep the flow of products and services moving.

Important terms and concepts

distribution in the marketing mix:
  p. 139
channel of distribution: p. 139
physical distribution: p. 141
logistics: p. 141
order processing: p. 142
materials handling: p. 142
warehousing: p. 142
distribution centre: p. 143
inventory management: p. 143
just-in-time: p. 143
transport: p. 143
railways: p. 144

motor vehicles: p. 144
air freight: p. 144
water transport: p. 144
pipelines: p. 144
transit time: p. 145
reliability: p. 145
capability: p. 145
accessibility: p. 145
security: p. 145
traceability: p. 145
marketing intermediaries: p. 146
direct-marketing channel: p. 146
agents: p. 147

Case Study: Retailer profits at heart of Musgrave retailer service strategy

Musgrave Retailer Services has one aim to partner with independent retailers and help build profitable businesses. Cash and carries continue to play a vital role in the independent retail industry. According to John Callaghan, Musgrave's cash and carry director 'centralised distribution networks, real time stocktaking are concepts that are supposed to have finished off the cash and carry business long ago, but, cash and carry is still the dominant part of our business'.

The cash and carry is also a source of up-to-the minute information about new products and sales opportunities. Musgrave's cash and carry outlets strive to be even more to their customers. They carry 21,000 lines. The staff get to know their customers and understand their needs. For some customers the weekly trip to the cash and carry can be a brief respite from the constant pressure of being an independent retailer. Top of Musgrave's cash and carry priorities for remaining at number one cash and carry in Ireland is availability of product. Customers need to be able to rely on getting what they need. Maintaining strong relationships with customers is also a key.

To stay competitive, companies need to strive constantly to remove costs and inefficiencies. As part of its re-brand Musgrave has made its cash and carries more efficient by dividing retail and food service products into separate areas. Now customers who are short on time can get in and out quicker. Musgrave also offer customers a choice of cash and carry or delivered service, and the option of dipping into both as the need arises. The two services are seen to complement each other and offer the right service to independent retailers of all sizes.

Musgrave's delivery service also offers a full technology-based solution which will not only receive electronic orders but manage the price files for the retailers. Musgrave's manage the master file for each order, allowing retailers to automatically update their systems with price changes. Musgrave offer a comprehensive package which includes warehouse distribution, a central billing package, full advice and training on topics such as fresh food, technology support, marketing activity and promotions that suit the needs of the business.

According to Paul Kerrigan, Musgrave, convenience retail director, 'Helping retailers to remain competitive is at the heart of both the delivered and cash and carry wings of Musgrave Retailer Services. The long term future of independent retailers mainly depends on their drive and ambition, and the independent retailers need support and partnership in today's environment'.

While Musgrave aims to support independent retailers, they do not have any ambitions to control them or compromise their autonomy because according to Callaghan 'independent retailers are just independent. They want control, they want to use their entrepreneurial skills and get ideas from the range, rather than just pushing the wheel, a lot of independent retailers like inventing the wheel'.

Source: http://www.checkout.ie

Case Study: Dubarry's e-Business project

Dubarry, the footwear brand of choice in the international sailing world has created a web site which not only cuts the administrative load of dealing with 18 international distributors, but for the first time enables it to build a relationship directly with its consumer base. Dubarry's website features a comprehensive business-to-business section, which streamlines the ordering process for distributors and allows them to do it online. The site also sells products to overseas consumers unable to buy locally the company's market leading marine footwear collection and its sister 'outdoor' collection.

According to Marketing Director, Michael Walsh the company thoroughly researched the market before developing their own website. Dubarry also took a very close look at its own business and how it is segmented. It literally sketched a matrix, which looked at the business both geographically and in product areas. From their background research, the company identified three very clear strategies – a business to business aimed at its international distributors; a business to consumer element aimed at consumers in areas where it did not have market representation and a more general aim to promote and assist in the marketing of the brand whether to consumer or trade. Initially, their distributors were concerned that Dubarry would sell across their territories and were very resistant to the website. In order to reassure their distributors they took a policy decision not to sell into markets where they had an existing presence.

The website which was eventually created is organised primarily according to geographic region. According to Walsh 'We needed to take different product categories and regions into account. Not just the Irish market, the UK market and the rest of the world where we had representation. But the areas where we didn't have representation – they were particularly important'. With the online system Dubarry has saved itself a substantial amount of time and effort in processing distributor orders, largely because they system will not allow distributors to order product when it is not available. The system is capable of blanking out what is not available at a particular time. With all of their distributors online, the new system saves them time and effort too.

While the company has committed to not selling into markets where an existing distributor is in place it is however planning to offer specific items, which local distributors are not supplying. If a distributor decides not to stock a product from the Dubarry collection, the company are not going to deprive someone in Australia, for example, from buying it. This serves two purposes, it motivates the distributor to provide full representation of the range and equally it allows the distributor to go to retailers and let them know that they will not be listed on the website as a stockist of a particular item. According to Walsh 'That's important to us because it gives us control. It means we know what is happening in distribution. There's a comfort factor initially for distributors because we're not cutting across their territory but we will if they don't perform'. On a practical level, the company is receiving enquiries from potential distributors in areas where it does not yet have representation. It has decided to include a section for these inquiries on its business-to-business section of the website. The final aspect of the site is brand building as Dubarry have built a brand that now has achieved world wide recognition within a sailing niche.

Source: http://www.enterprise-ireland.com/ebusiness/case-studies

Questions for review

1. What are the main elements of the physical distribution mix?
2. Compare direct and intermediary distribution.
3. Discuss the purpose of a physical distribution system.
4. List the various transport options available to a company, giving the advantages and disadvantages of each method.
5. Write a brief description of (*a*) intensive distribution, (*b*) selective distribution, and (*c*) exclusive distribution.
6. What are the main factors a marketing manager needs to consider when selecting distribution channels?

10
MARKETING COMMUNICATION

Chapter objectives

After reading this chapter you should be able to
- define the marketing communication process and its elements
- explain the communication mix and the uniqueness of each tool
- describe the steps involved in developing a communication programme
- identify the factors that affect the selection of the communication mix.

10.1 *The marketing communication process*

According to Dibb et al. (1997), marketing communication can be defined as 'the communication of information which facilitates or expedites the exchange process.' Marketing communication (promotion) is the fourth element in the marketing mix. This comprises a mix of tools available to the marketer, called the *communications mix,* which consists of personal selling, advertising, sales promotion, and public relations (see fig. 10.1).

The communications mix is the direct way in which a company attempts to communicate with a variety of target audiences. The mix can be used to
- inform potential customers about the benefits of the product
- persuade customers to use the product
- remind customers of the benefits of using the product.

Communication is the sharing of meaning between sender and receiver. There are eight *elements* in the *marketing communication process*:

(1) Source

The source (sender) of the message will be the company with a product or service to offer to a target (receiver). It is the source that instigates the communication process. A source could be, for example, a marketing manager who wishes to communicate a message to thousands of consumers through an advertisement.

(2) Message

The message is what the source wants the audience to know or understand as a result of receiving the communication. It may be any combination of words, pictures, or symbols.

(3) Receiver

Consumers who read, hear or see the message are the receivers (the target audience).

(4) Channel

The message is communicated by means of a communication channel, such as television, radio, print, or personal selling.

(5) Encoding

Encoding is the process of having the source transform an idea or intended message into a set of symbols.

(6) Decoding

Decoding is the reverse of encoding. It involves having the receiver take a set of symbols—the message—and transform them back into an idea. Individual receivers tend to interpret incoming messages very differently, depending on their attitudes, values, and beliefs.

(7) Feedback

Feedback is how the receiver responds to the message, for example carrying out market research to find out how successful the message has been. With mass communication, such as television advertising, feedback tends to be slow and difficult to collect. It may be so delayed or distorted that it is of no use to the source.

(8) Noise

When the result of decoding is different from what was coded, noise exists. Noise includes all activity and influences that distract from any aspect of the communication process between the source and receiver. Noise can be background traffic, people talking, distracting music, or the intended receiver being distracted from watching television when the advertisement is broadcast.

10.2 *The communications mix*

To communicate to consumers, a company may use one or more of four communication tools: advertising, sales promotion, personal selling, and public relations. A ***communications mix*** is the combination of two or more of the tools a company chooses to use.

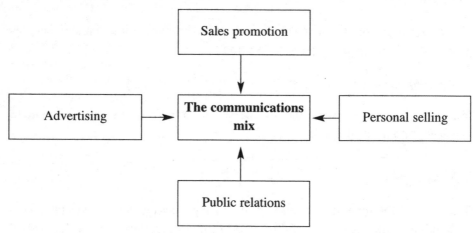

Fig. 10.1: *The tools of the communications mix*

Advertising

Kotler et.al., (2003) defines advertising as 'any paid form of nonpersonal presentation and promotion of ideas, goods or services through mass media such as newspapers, magazines, television or radio by an identified sponsor.'

Advertising has a very wide scope. When someone places a card in a local newsagent's window announcing an item for sale, this is an advertisement. This can be contrasted with a large company's commercial shown on television. Each of these examples may be successful if it achieves its objective, namely moving potential customers closer to the point of purchase for a particular product or service.

Advertising usually involves mass media, such as radio, television, cinema, magazines, and the Internet. There are many factors that should be considered before advertising is undertaken. Advertisements should first be considered as part of the total communication process. The objectives, message and likely budget may well have been determined. Decisions now have to be taken on the role of advertising as part of the promotional mix. Primarily, it revolves around the balance between advertising and personal selling, as these are usually the elements where most money is committed.

Before an advertising message is made public, a company or marketer should carry out marketing research (see chapter 5). The research will enable the company to make sure the proposed message will be understood by the target market and that the target market will actually see the medium chosen. *Competitive advertising* is concerned with emphasising the special features of the product or brand as a means of outselling competition. Usually the seller seeks to communicate the unique benefits, real or imaginary, that distinguishes the product and gives it its competitive edge. Given that most markets are mature and often crowded, this type of advertising is very common and very important.

Comparative advertising means making direct comparison between one product and another, showing the advertiser's product in a much more favourable light, of course. Alternatively, the comparison may be more subtle, referring to 'other leading brands' and leaving it up to the target audience to decide which rival product is intended.

Advantages of advertising

- It communicates to the mass audience a product's features, benefits, and competitive advantage.
- It benefits a company by contributing to a strong long-term corporate image.
- It can help to create awareness and to build image and attitudes through reminders.
- It can reinforce positive attitudes through reminders.
- It supports the other tools of the communication mix by creating awareness, thereby helping salespeople.
- It helps to reduce sales fluctuations, which may be influenced by seasonal demand.
- It facilitates the repetition of a message many times over.

Disadvantages of advertising

- It can be very costly to produce and to advertise a message, particularly on television.
- It does not provide direct feedback, which makes it difficult for marketers to know how well a message was received.
- It is impersonal and not as persuasive as personal selling.

Advertising media

Advertising media are called on to perform the task of delivering the message to the consumer. The advertiser needs, therefore, to select the medium or media most appropriate to the task in hand, given their relative effectiveness and the budget available.

Radio

On the positive side:
- Low cost
- Can target specific audience
- Advertisements can be placed quickly
- Can use sound and humour effectively.

On the negative side:
- Cannot handle complex messages
- No visual excitement
- Short exposure time
- Commercial clutter.

Television

On the positive side:
- Can target specific audience
- Excellent for demonstrating product usage
- Digital TV will open up interactive opportunities
- Uses picture, print, sound and motion for effect
- Ability to reach a wide diverse audience.

On the negative side:
- High campaign cost
- Long lead times needed for production
- Commercial clutter
- Long-term advertiser commitments
- Short life of message.

Outdoor media

On the positive side:
- Moderate cost
- Geographic selectivity

- High visibility
- Opportunity for repeat exposures
- Flexibility.

On the negative side:
- Message must be short and simple
- Lack of demographic selectivity
- Visual clutter
- Subject to damage and defacement
- Traffic hazard or eyesore.

Direct Mail

On the positive side:
- Advert can be saved
- Easy to measure performance
- Highly selective
- Circulation controlled by advertiser
- Personal
- Very flexible, 3-D, pop-up advertisements etc.

On the negative side:
- Expensive
- Considered junk mail by many people
- No editorial matter to attract readers
- Invasion of privacy.

Press

On the positive side:
- Can target specific audiences
- Handles detail well
- Advertisements can be placed and changed
- Advertisements can be clipped and saved
- Can convey complex information.

On the negative side:
- Limited control of advertisement position
- Can be low impact
- Timing difficulties in coordinating appearance of the advertisement.

Internet

On the positive side:
- International communication opportunities
- Allows the user to interact with the marketer online
- Market research information can be obtained from people using the site.

On the negative side:
- Security, consumers giving a credit card number that can be intercepted by someone else
- Websites need to be maintained and updated, users will become frustrated if information is out of date
- Lack of clarity on who is browsing the web.

Sales promotion

A second promotional tool is sales promotion. This is a short-term inducement of value offered to stimulate interest in buying a product or service. The British Advertising Standards Authority defines sales promotion as 'those marketing techniques, which are used, usually on a temporary basis, to make goods and services more attractive to the consumer by providing some additional benefit whether in cash or in kind.'

Sales promotions are usually used in conjunction with advertising or personal selling and are rarely used in isolation. They are offered to retailers and to salespeople as well as to ultimate consumers.

Sales promotion methods

(a) Consumer sales promotion methods:

- Banded packs, e.g. toothbrush banded to a toothpaste at a reduced price for the two combined
- Money-off coupons
- Premium offers, e.g. items offered free or at a minimum cost
- Stamp collecting schemes, e.g. SuperValu promotions
- Free sample or tasting offers
- In-store demonstrations
- Point-of-sale displays
- Competitions
- Personality promotions

(b) Trade sales promotion methods:

- Buying allowances, e.g. temporary price reduction for buying certain quantities of a product
- Free merchandise
- Competitions
- Trade shows
- Exhibitions
- Bonuses
- Business meetings
- Sales contests
- Store demonstrations
- Advertising allowance

Advantages of sales promotion

- The short-term nature of these promotions often stimulates sales for their duration.
- They arouse attention and provide information.
- They offer value to the consumer, for example in the form of a money-off coupon or rebate, which provides an incentive to buy.
- They boost sales by persuading regular customers to bring forward their purchases.

Disadvantages of sales promotion

- Their gains are short-term.
- To build long-term brand preference they need advertising support.
- They lose their effectiveness if they are conducted continuously.
- They are expensive.

Personal selling

Personal selling is any paid form of interpersonal presentation of products and services. In contrast to advertising, personal selling involves face-to-face communication between the source (sender) and receiver (target audience). Murray and O'Driscoll (1998) view personal selling as 'perhaps the most powerful, certainly the most sophisticated, and often the most expensive element of the communication mix.'

The personal sales approach is the more direct and potent way of selling many products. It ranges from door-to-door insurance salespeople to assistants in a department store. Companies spend large sums of money training their salespeople in selling processes.

Personal selling processes consists of the following steps:

(1) developing a list of potential customers
(2) pre-approach preparation
(3) approaching the customer
(4) presentation and demonstration
(5) dealing with feedback
(6) closing the sale
(7) follow-up.

With advances in technology, personal selling also takes place by phone and through electronic mail.

Firms can choose between a hard sell approach and a soft sell approach

Hard sell strategies:

- Concern for self
- Talking
- Pushing product
- Presenting features
- Advocating without acknowledging

Soft sell strategies:

- Concern for customer
- Questions for discussion
- Listening
- Providing buying opportunity
- Presenting benefits
- Acknowledging needs

Advantages of personal selling

- A sales representative can direct presentations at specific target sectors, thereby reducing wasted coverage.
- The salesperson can interpret the potential customer's reaction to the message.
- The feedback is immediate and allows the salesperson to modify the message accordingly.
- It is very useful for complex or technical products or services.

Disadvantages of personal selling

- It is the most expensive tool of the communications mix.
- It requires long-term commitment.

- It may lead to inconsistent communication to customers, as the sales-persons can change the message.

Public relations

Public relations (PR) deals with the quality and nature of the relationship between a company and its various 'publics'. These may include customers, shareholders, employees, suppliers, the Government, the media, and pressure groups. According to Dibb et al. (1997), public relations is 'the planned and sustained effort to establish and maintain goodwill and mutual understanding between a company and its publics.' As with any marketing activity, managers must be sure that PR integrates with the rest of the organisation's promotional efforts, and that it is clearly related to wider company objectives.

Marketing PR may be used for long-term strategic image building, developing credibility and raising the organisation's profile, to enhance marketing activities. When used this way, it becomes a planned element of the wider promotional mix, working in synergy with the others. A new product launch, or the introduction of a big new innovative advertising campaign, for instance, might benefit from planned PR aimed at specific audiences through specific media to generate interest and awareness.

Corporate PR may be used as part of a long-term relationship building strategy with various publics or as a short-term tactical response to unforeseen crisis. Short-term circumstances are somewhat unpredictable, and therefore any organisation needs to have contingency plans ready so that a well-rehearsed crisis management team can go into action as soon as disaster strikes. This means, for example, that everyone should know who will be responsible for collating information and feeding it to the media, and that senior management will be properly briefed and trained to face media interrogation. Such measures result in the organisation being seen to handle the crisis capably and efficiently, and also reduce the chances of different spokespersons innocently contradicting each other, or of the media being kept short of information because everyone thinks that someone else is dealing with that aspect.

Public relations encompasses the following techniques and activities:

Publicity: This is a form of promotion that is not paid for directly. It is conducted through press statements, press conferences, press briefings, and press receptions.

Events: A company may hold functions or social events, such as annual general meetings, factory tours, and special parties on its premises for its employees, customers, and at times the general public.

Advertising: This concentrates on establishing and reinforcing a company's image.

Publications: These include written materials such as annual reports, brochures, company newsletters, magazines and audio-visual materials such as promotional DVDs, recruitment DVDs, websites and CDs.

Lobbying: This is an exercise by which public relations practitioners try to influence decision-makers in the development and implementation of various policies.

Internal communication: It is important for a company to keep its internal public—its employees—informed at all times. To achieve this it may use a house journal or newsletter, staff meetings or briefings, electronic bulletin boards, and an intranet.

Crisis management: The co-ordinated effort to handle the effects of unfavourable publicity, ensuring fast and accurate communication in times of emergency.

Sponsorship: The financial or material support of an event, person, organisation, group or product by private individuals or organisations. It is given with the expectation of a benefit in return. An organisation can communicate with its target audiences through sponsorship.

Advantages of public relations

- It can support and complement other marketing activities.
- It is much more credible and convincing than advertisements.
- It often communicates messages to selected publics and generally influences opinion more effectively than advertising.

Disadvantages of public relations

- There is no guarantee that a press statement or photograph will be published by a target newspaper.
- Effective public relations does not happen easily and so requires long-term planning.

10.3 *Developing a communication programme*

Step 1: Identifying the target audience

The marketing manager must decide who exactly the target audience (receiver) is for the communication programme, for example, the target audience may be children. The target audience may also be potential or existing customers and may be made up of individuals, groups, or the general public. The type of audience chosen will influence the message, how it will be transmitted, when it will be transmitted, where it will be transmitted, and who will transmit it.

Step 2: Defining the communication objectives

Once the target audience has been selected, the company must decide on the objectives of the programme. This means it has to define what responses it is looking for, for example, it needs to know what stage of the 'product adoption process' the consumer is at and to what stage he or she needs to be moved. The stages of the **product adoption process** include (1) **awareness**—the person becomes aware that a product exists but has little information about it; (2) **interest**—the person seeks information about the product; (3) **evaluation**—the consumer decides whether the product will meet their individual needs; (4) **trial**—the consumer uses or experiences the product for the first time; and (5) **adoption**—the consumer decides to make full and regular use of the product.

The purpose of the programme therefore is to move the consumer along these stages to the adoption process. For a communication programme to be successful, the objectives must be precise, practical, and measurable.

Step 3: Choosing a message

The next step in the communication programme is developing what the actual message should be. A marketer must decide on the content, structure and form of the message, that is, what the company wants to say, how it will say it, and what sight, sound, colour or other stimuli it will use.

Step 4: Selecting the media

The marketing manager can decide what channel or channels of communication to use to get the message to the desired audience so that the objectives set out in step 2 can be achieved. There are two types: **personal communication channels**, for example face-to-face, telephone, word of mouth, salespeople, well-known personalities, and opinion leaders, and **impersonal communication channels**, for example print media, television and radio, signs, posters, and the world wide web.

Step 5: Deciding on a budget

It is important that a company develops a realistic budget so that it can achieve its objectives. It is difficult to determine this amount, because there is no way to measure the precise effects of investing in a promotion.

There are four ways of deciding on how much a company should spend on promoting its product or service:

- the *affordable method*—where the budget is set at what the company can afford
- the *percentage of sales method*—where the budget is set at a certain proportion of current or future sales
- the *competitive-parity method*—where the budget is set to match or exceed what the competition is spending on promotion
- the *objective and task method*—where the budget is based on the analysis and costing of the communication objectives and tasks.

Step 6: Selecting the communication mix

Once the budget has been developed, the next step is to divide it among the tools of the communication mix. The company can select its communication mix by analysing each of the tools individually (see section 10.2).

Step 7: Implementing and evaluating results

This step involves putting the communication plan into action. To produce new brochures, for example, a company will invest time and effort in drafting, designing and producing this communication plan. The communication plan must then be implemented in accordance with the company's objectives, and its progress must be monitored against what was originally proposed. Finally, gathering information by means of marketing research (qualitative and quantitative) may be used to assess the performance of the communication plan.

10.4 Selecting a communication mix

When developing a communication programme, the marketing manager has to select a communication mix that achieves the company's objectives within a defined budget. This will determine whether it is appropriate to use advertising as opposed to personal selling, or whether the company should use a combination of the communication tools. To do this the company needs to be aware of the factors that affect the selection of a communication mix. These are as follows:

- The company's *communication objectives*: awareness of the product (refer to step 1 of the communication programme above).
- Budget and resources: This determines the available budget and if the company has adequate resources to employ the communication tool (or tools).
- Type of market: If the company is dealing with a consumer market it should use mass communication, that is, advertising; if it is an industrial market it should use personal selling.
- *Communication strategy*: This can be either a push strategy or a pull strategy (described in chapter 9).

The following quotation from Kotler (1999) sums up the role of marketing communication in relation to the marketing mix: 'Although the promotion mix is the company's primary communication activity, the entire marketing mix— *promotion, product, price and place*—must be co-ordinated for the greatest communication impact.'

10.5 *Integrated marketing communications (IMC)*

Ideally, marketing communications from each communication mix element (advertising, sales promotions, advertising and public relations) should be integrated. In other words, the message reaching the consumer should be the same regardless of whether it is from a TV advertisement, a salesperson, a newspaper article or a free sample in a supermarket. Unfortunately, this is not always the case. When planning communication programmes, many marketers fail to integrate their communication efforts from one element of the mix to the next.

This unintegrated approach to marketing communication has propelled more companies to adopt the concept of **integrated marketing communications/ IMC**. IMC is the method of carefully co-ordinating all promotional activities – advertising, sales promotions, personal selling and public relations, as well as sponsorship, direct marketing and other forms of promotion – to produce a consistent, unified message that is customer focused. Marketing managers carefully work out the roles the various marketing communication tools will play in the marketing mix. The timing of various marketing communication activities is co-ordinated and the results of each campaign are carefully monitored to improve future use of the promotional mix elements. Normally, a marketing communications director is appointed. He/she has overall responsibility for integrating the company's marketing communications. Hewlett-Packard, for example, created 'marketing councils' within the company to devise strategies by which all marketing messages flow for both current campaigns and new product launches.

Important terms and concepts

marketing communication process: p. 154

communications mix: p. 154

elements of the marketing communication process: p. 154

tools of the communications mix: p. 156

advertising: p. 156

competitive advertising: p. 157

comparative advertising: p. 157

advertising media: p. 158

sales promotion: p. 160

hard sell strategies: p. 162

soft sell strategies: p. 162

personal selling: p. 162

public relations: p. 163

marketing PR: p. 163

corporate PR: p. 163

developing a communication programme: p. 164

product adoption process: p. 165

awareness: p. 165

interest: p. 165

evaluation: p. 165

trial: p. 165

adoption: p. 165

personal communication channel: p. 165

impersonal communication channel: p. 165

affordable method: p. 166

percentage of sales method: p. 166

competitive-parity method: p. 166

objective and task method: p. 166

selecting a communication mix: p. 166

communication objectives: p. 167

communication strategy: p. 167

integrated marketing communications (IMC): p. 167

Case Study: Sponsorship and the promotional mix: Budweiser

Budweiser – the leading beer in the Irish take home market – was launched in Ireland in 1985 when Guinness (now Diageo) was given the licence to brew and market the beer from the Anheuser-Busch company. It became an instant hit in both draft and packaged. The brand marketed itself as a 'fun' brand and

because of that it has sponsored events such as SuperBowl Parties and Fourth of July parties. Its advertising has also focused on sports and fun including its campaign 'Over there, over here' which has 'humour' and 'fun' at its core. But sponsorship, albeit expensive, can be huge in terms of gaining new customers. Budweiser have been sponsoring the Irish Derby since 1985, and the Budweiser name is now synonymous with that event.

Budweiser sponsored the football World Cup which took place in Germany in June 2006. Very importantly for the sponsor, the matches were all shown in the late afternoon and early evening on TV. That made the sponsorship of the event by Budweiser much more valuable in an Irish context. It gave Budweiser pitch signage and a lot of activity in Germany. It also gave the world's biggest beer the first refusal of broadcast sponsorship, similar to the sponsorship by the brand of the Premiership show on RTE. Budweiser secured the sponsorship on RTE of all matches. This was seen as a great coup for the brand as RTE showed every World Cup match. Budweiser also secured sponsorship of coverage on ITV, so wherever one was going to watch the World Cup – whether it be on RTE or ITV, Budweiser was there at the 'top and tail' of all the adverts.

According to Niall Tracey, marketing manager for Budweiser in Ireland, 'For fans of the game, watching the game and drinking a beer is one of the key drinking occasions. We want to make Budweiser synonymous with watching the game. So that when you're watching a game – whether in the pub or at home, the beer that naturally fits with that is Bud.' To achieve this Budweiser produced World Cup packs, consisting of 10- and 15-bottle packs and the 12-can packs, featuring a 'Text to Win' competition which could have had fans 'drinking a Bud, watching the game' at the actual game in Germany. The idea was that World Cup fans would send in a phone photo of themselves watching the game and Budweiser would send the lucky winners to Germany on an all-expenses paid trip. The result was a surge in sales of Budweiser right through the summer as new consumers tried out the beer to participate in the World Cup promotion and continued to purchase through June with the second promotion based on promotional prices.

The reason why Budweiser gets so heavily involved in sponsorship is that it carries the 'passion' of its consumers. It knows that people are passionate about many things, usually sport or music and that when Budweiser supports those events and brings passion to life, consumers appreciate Budweiser getting involved and reward it with their loyalty.

Source: http://www.checkout.ie

Case Study: Petrol promotions pumps up the profits: Superquinn

In order to attract more customers, Superquinn joined forces with forecourt operator Maxol. The deal, which gave customers €2 off every €20 of fuel at Maxol for every €50 spent at Superquinn, followed a similar partnership between Dunnes and Texaco and Tesco's rock-bottom prices at its forecourt outlets. The Superquinn/Maxol deal ran for a period of eight weeks, in which participating customers received a card-style voucher when they spent €50 on groceries at Superquinn, which could then be redeemed at any Maxol station in Ireland.

It was a great offer for all motorists. The deal brought together two of the leading Irish family-owned businesses who had a strong reputation for high quality and excellent service, and in particular, value for money. Although popular in Ireland, the use of petrol as a promotional tool, either through company-owned service stations or partnership deals is also common in other European markets. In Spain, Carrefour had a promotion which gave a 10% discount on petrol spend of €30 or more. However, this trend of petrol promotions and price reductions has decreased in particular in the UK, where increasing oil prices have pushed up prices at the supermarket-owned petrol stations.

Source: Checkout Ireland

Questions for review

1. What are the elements of the marketing communication process?
2. Discuss each tool of the communications mix. Illustrate your response with examples.
3. Describe the steps involved in developing a communication programme.
4. What factors affect the selection of the communications mix?
5. Think of a product or service with which you are familiar. Identify the tools used to promote it.

BIBLIOGRAPHY

Abell, D. (1980), *Defining the Business: The Starting Point of Strategic Planning,* Englewood Cliffs (NJ): Prentice-Hall.

Baker, M. (1990), *Dictionary of Marketing and Advertising,* London: Macmillan.

Bennett, P.D. (1988), *Marketing Terms,* Chicago: American Marketing Association, p. 189.

Dibb, S., Simkin, L., Pride, W. and Ferrell, O. (1997), *Marketing Concepts and Strategies,* New York: Houghton Mifflin.

Dibbenbach, J. (1983), 'Corporate environmental analysis in large US corporations', *Long Range Planning,* vol. 16, no. 3, pp. 107–16.

Harrell, G. D. (2002), *Marketing — Connecting with Customers,* New Jersey: Prentice Hall.

Kotler, P. and Armstrong, G. (2003), *Marketing: An Introduction* (sixth edition), Englewood Cliffs (NJ): Prentice-Hall.

Kotler, P., Armstrong, G., Saunders, J. and Wong, V. (2002), *Principles of Marketing* (fourth European edition), London: Prentice-Hall.

Langer, E. and Imba, L. (1980), 'The role of mindlessness in the perception of deviance', *Journal of Personality and Social Psychology,* vol. 38, pp. 360–7.

MacDonald, M. (1989), 'Ten barriers to marketing planning,' *Journal of Marketing Management,* vol. 5 (1), 1–8.

Mitchell, A. (1999), 'Marketers must grasp the Net or face oblivion', *Marketing Week,* 18 February, 30–1.

Mowen, J. (1995), *Consumer Behavior* (fourth edition), Englewood Cliffs (NJ): Prentice-Hall.

Murray, J. and O'Driscoll, A. (1998), *Managing Marketing: Concepts and Irish Cases,* Dublin: Gill & Macmillan.

Page, S. (1995), *Introductory Marketing,* Cheltenham: Stanley Thornes.

Peters, T. (1988), *Thriving on Chaos,* New York: Pan.

Porter, M. (1980), *Competitive Strategy: Techniques for Analysing Industries and Competitors,* New York: Free Press.

Ries, A. (1995), 'What's in a name?' *Sales and Marketing Management,* October, 36–7.

Ries, A. and Trout, J. (1981), *Positioning: The Battle for Your Mind,* London: McGraw-Hill.

Robinson, P.J., Farris, C.W. and Wind, Y. (1967) *Industrial Buying Behaviour and Creative Marketing,* London: Allyn and Bacon.

Tull, D. and Hawkins, D. (1992), *Industrial Marketing Research,* London: Kogan Page.

Wind, Y. (1984), 'Going to market: new twists for some old tricks', *Wharton Magazine,* 4.

Zikmund, W. and d'Amico, M. (1996), *Marketing* (fifth edition), New York: West.